OVER GUILT AND S
ST TEMPTATION ST
AS A RIGHTEOUS R
F FEAR STAND THR
IP STAND IN FORGIVENESS STAND IN LOVE STAND I
STAND IN PATIENCE STAND IN KINDNESS STAND IN
HFULNESS STAND IN GENTLENESS STAND IN SELF-C
RFULLY STAND AS A MAN STAND AS A WOMAN STAN
AS A FRIEND STAND IN FAMILY STAND AS A REBEL S
ATION STAND IN TIMES OF TESTING STAND IN WAT
UNION ST   RE STAND
POWER C   TH STAN
IPTURE ST   WHEN D
DESPITE   ND WHEN
OVER GU   IDST OF C
ST TEMPT   RY STAN

STAND

A **call** to **uncompromising witness**
& **discipleship** through journaling,
prayer & scripture—an **interactive**
journey to the **heart of Jesus.**

By Ben Johnson & Jeremy Postal

HFULNES   IN SELF-C
RFULLY STAND AS A MAN STAND AS A WOMAN STAN
AS A FRIEND STAND IN FAMILY STAND AS A REBEL S
ATION STAND IN TIMES OF TESTING STAND IN WAT
UNION STAND FOR JESUS STAND IN CULTURE STAND
POWER OF THE HOLY SPIRIT STAND IN FAITH STAN
IPTURE STAND DEVOTIONALS STAND EVEN WHEN D
DESPITE WORRY STAND WHEN HURT STAND WHEN
OVER GUILT AND SHAME STAND IN THE MIDST OF C
ST TEMPTATION STAND DOWN WHEN ANGRY STAN
AS A RIGHTEOUS REBEL STAND THROUGH REJECTIO
F FEAR STAND THROUGH UNCERTAINTY STAND WI
IP STAND IN FORGIVENESS STAND IN LOVE STAND I

NEXT GENERATION MINISTRIES | BC-YUKON PENTECOSTAL ASSEMBLIES OF CANADA

STAND

Copyright © 2012 by Ben Johnson and Jeremy Postal

Requests for information should be addressed to:

Ben Johnson
Next Generation Ministries BC-Yukon PAOC
20411 Douglas Crescent
Langley, BC
CANADA V3A 1Z5

Phone: 604-533-2232
E-mail: info@historymaker.ca

**Web Site: historymaker.ca
nextgenerationministries.ca**

CONTENTS

INTRODUCTION

» " … Be strong in the Lord and in his mighty power. Put on all of God's armor so that you will be able to stand firm against all strategies of the devil. For we are not fighting against flesh-and-blood enemies, but against evil rulers and authorities of the unseen world, against mighty powers in this dark world, and against evil spirits in the heavenly places. Therefore, put on every piece of God's armor so you will be able to resist the enemy in the time of evil. Then after the battle you will still be standing firm. Stand your ground, putting on the belt of truth and the body armor of God's righteousness. For shoes, put on the peace that comes from the Good News so that you will be fully prepared. In addition to all of these, hold up the shield of faith to stop the fiery arrows of the devil. Put on salvation as your helmet, and take the sword of the Spirit, which is the word of God. Pray in the Spirit at all times and on every occasion. Stay alert and be persistent in your prayers for all believers everywhere." Ephesians 6:10-18

We are in a spiritual war. This is a reality for followers of Christ, whether we are aware of it or not. We are in the midst of a life and death battle. Step back with me for a second and observe what is really going on in this world: the casualties, the broken hearts, the loneliness, the hurt, the brokenness. As we come to know God and His Word more and more, we must live as though the spiritual battle is more real than the part of reality we can actually see. This is a war zone we live in, and there is no escaping it.

The writer of Ephesians calls us as soldiers in the war to **"STAND."** We are called to prepare ourselves for this spiritual war with spiritual armour and weapons. It might seem quite the brave task to be expected to fight and **STAND** in a war zone and our natural desire might be to go against such a call, seeking something much more comfortable and low-risk. We'd probably rather be relaxing on a beach in Maui or spending the day at Disneyland. Truth be told we'd probably rather be doing almost anything rather than engaging in warfare. Why would we sign up for a war? But the reality is we are in this battle, whether we signed up for it or not.

Before you become overwhelmed with the reality of this, the good news is that God has given us the power and the ability to take a **STAND**. We have everything necessary to fight the good fight. Jesus has ultimately won the war, but while we are still here on earth, there are spiritual battles that must be fought every day. God has given you armour, weapons, gifts, and, most importantly, His Holy Spirit to enable you to fight the good fight of faith and take your **STAND**. He has called and empowered you to win in every area of your life.

Maybe you are reading this right now and are unsure about whose side of the fight you're on. Maybe you haven't decided to make Jesus the leader of your life. Or maybe, at one time in your life, you felt closer to God but you know that you are not in a right relationship with Him today.

Maybe you are feeling stirred right now, sensing His call upon your life to follow Him in a fresh and radical way. The awesome thing is that His grace is reaching out to you right now. What you are feeling is the love and conviction of the Holy Spirit. He is convincing you of your extreme need for Jesus, drawing you to Him. You don't have to wait; you can respond right now and choose to **STAND** for Christ! You can be assured that from this day forward you have a brand new start.

The Bible says that we are all born separated from God because of sin. We literally miss God's mark. There's no way we can work to be a good person and be acceptable to God, because we all fall short of God's standard. Fortunately, there is also no sin too big that God can't forgive. The good news, or "the Gospel" message, is that Jesus came to pay the price for all of our sins! He came to make us right with God. He came from Heaven, lived as a man, and was tempted in every way that we are, yet Jesus did not sin. He never missed God's mark. He died on a cross so that you don't have to die—He died in your place. He actually beat death, and rose from the grave to give you and I the privilege and gift of knowing Him personally and having His power fill our lives every day! Without the power of God in our lives, we could never **STAND**. But with His power, and because of His grace, we can live our lives with freedom, passion and purpose.

Before you read any further, pray this prayer from your heart:

Jesus,
I come to You right now and confess that I need You in my life. I believe You are the Son of God and that You died for me on a cross, rose again, and are alive today. Come into the centre of my life, Jesus, and make me a new person. Forgive me of all my sins, failures and mistakes. Wash me clean and make me right with You. Today I choose to make You the king and leader of my life. Help me to live for You and for Your cause all of my days. Thank You for saving me and giving my life purpose and a brand new start. Amen.

If you have prayed this prayer from your heart, you are now ready to begin to take your **STAND.** We would love to hear from you. Please contact us and let us know what you did today. **Email us at prayer@historymaker.ca or Tweet us at @historymakerbc** We will be praying for you and will be cheering you on all the way!

My prayer as you read through this journal and use its practical resources and exercises is that you would be personally transformed. I pray that you might learn something, but even more that you would draw closer to God, be empowered by the presence of the Holy Spirit inside of you, and that you would **STAND** as a Historymaker effectively fighting for, reaching and leading your generation.

STANDING With You,
Ben Johnson

INVITATION
TO STAND

» My first guitar, at least the first one I (Jeremy) can remember, was a hand-me-down that had seen a lot of rock shows and back alley busking. The guitar had dings and nicks and gouges over its entire body and there were even a few lighter burns for good measure. Even if the guitar hadn't been painted bright blue, it would have still stood out where ever it went.

I loved that guitar and it was my first real attempt at becoming a "guitarer." I practiced scales and power chording and I dreamed about playing rock and roll on some stage in some city I wouldn't remember the next day. I was certain I was going to become the next Jimmy Page and that my life would be filled with music, record contracts, and autograph sessions.

There was only one problem: learning to play the guitar took a lot of time and energy and I didn't really feel like putting in the work. In the end I'm not sure what happened to that beautiful old guitar; I might have left it somewhere or, more likely, it found its way to a home where it would be better used.

My second guitar was slightly different. This time someone handed me an electric guitar and told me to practice. And practice I would, if I could fit it in between snowboarding, skateboarding, chopping wood, or doing anything else. I was proud of that guitar and it actually sounded good, but the problem was I couldn't make it sound that way. I don't know what happened to that guitar either but I have my suspicions about who took it. To be honest though, I can't blame them. That guitar should have been freed to be played by someone who could make it sound like what it was supposed to sound like.

My third guitar was given to me as well. The musician who gave it to me has a big record contract and really inspired me to give guitaring a go this time. At this point in my life, I was living in a van in the desert and it made sense to have an instrument to keep me company on those starry nights. It was an exciting time in my life as a guitarer; exciting because I would come up with any excuse not to play it. It was too hot, too cold, I was too tired, and it was out of tune. Eventually a visiting friend dropped in on my desert living quarters and took the guitar back home to Canada for me; I never saw it again.

Now, close to twenty-years after pursuing the guitar, I can still only play three chords that I tentatively creak out before answering people's question: "I didn't know you play guitar?" The truthful answer is "I don't." I really hoped I would, and I had big plans to play the guitar, but it just never really worked out like I thought it would. And even though I had a passion to play guitar (I could air guitar with the best of them!), I never had the deep conviction or the discipline to become highly skilled. I wanted to play the guitar—I didn't want to practice.

In many ways, following Jesus takes a similar approach. Many have dreams and plans and a huge passion to follow Jesus but often aren't intentional about being a good disciple. Maturing and growing as a disciple of Jesus requires that Christians are disciplined; this is discipleship. In the simplest sense of the word, discipleship is about following Jesus, modeling our lives after Him, and being shaped by the Holy Spirit to become more like Jesus. Discipleship is more than just coming to the front at a youth conference or a church service, it's really a decision to take a **STAND** and make Jesus number one in your life above all else. It's about living a life marked by a commitment to following Jesus.

Part of this commitment is about practicing different disciplines that grow and develop one's life as follower of Jesus. If you want to be a faithful disciple, there are different disciplines that you can practice to help you in your followership.

That said, practicing the different spiritual disciplines isn't something Christians must do. The crazy thing is that nothing changes how much God loves you. He loves you completely, fully, and probably more than any one of us will ever know. Rather, because God already loves us, the spiritual disciplines are something that we get to do as we love Him back and enjoy growing in our relationship with Him.

I've been working with youth and young adults for more than 15 years (Ben) and in some ways I'm quite optimistic about what is happening spiritually in Canadian young people. One of the things we see in this current generation is that many people seem to desire to know God. As leaders who have dedicated our lives to telling people about the love, grace and forgiveness of God, this is very encouraging. At the same time, it deeply grieves us to see that many people don't seem to fully comprehend what it truly means to take a courageous **STAND** as a follower of Jesus. To be a Christian the way Jesus has called us to be.

We hope that the words and spaces in this journal will help you discover some of what it means to follow Jesus well. While our hope is that you will learn many things about Jesus, our greatest desire is that you would come to know Christ in a more personal way.

Throughout the book you will find suggested spiritual disciplines that you can try out, sometimes by yourself and sometimes practiced with others. There are Bible stories to read, there is journaling space for you to write down prayers and thoughts, and there are stories and teaching about **STANDING** as a disciple in today's world.

Thanks for joining us as we look into how, as a generation of young Christians, we can **STAND** up and **STAND** out as followers of Jesus. We pray that as you read and work through the material in this book, you would learn to follow Jesus with a deeper, clearer and fuller understanding of what it means to be a disciple. Through this process we believe that not only will your spiritual life grow, but the lives of the people around you will be impacted by your life. It's time to take your **STAND!**

STANDING With You,
Ben Johnson & Jeremy Postal

» An abundance of "Jesuses" have taken over the modern landscape of Christian thought. Attempts to modernize the Biblical and historical Jesus have given us some humorous and, admittedly, some embarrassing depictions of Jesus. While some of these pictures of Jesus have proven to be quite loyal to His person, work, and divinity, too many others have been about as successful as a miracle diet pill.

The Bible is quite clear in its warnings to avoid teaching that depicts a Jesus other than the Jesus presented in Scripture. I am continually amazed at how creatively we tend to read our own culture back into the portrait of Jesus. I'll give you a few examples.

To begin with, there is the always-popular single, white, North American and totally employable Jesus who drives a mini-van and lives in the suburbs. This Jesus often pops up in paintings with blue eyes and boyish good looks.

The 1960s step-cousin to this Jesus is the hippie Jesus who wandered Palestine in a VW van—a homeless peasant with some quasi-intellectual thoughts and a few witty stories to entertain the people. Hippie-Jesus was non-confrontational, totally tolerant, and staged a few sit-ins just to show how tolerant and non-confrontational He was.

The opposite of Hippie-Jesus is the UFC-cage-fighter-Jesus currently being made popular by some modern leaders. This Jesus can take a beating, drinks beer, eats red meat, curses, worked a construction job, and will—in this world or the next—kick some tail.

And while Moralist-Jesus disapproves of UFC-Jesus drinking beer, He definitely agrees with Political-Lobbyist-Jesus that they need to put someone in a headlock.

Of course there is also Capitalist-Jesus, Che Guevara-Jesus, Jesus Christ Superstar-Jesus, Environmentalist-Jesus, and Oprah

Winfrey-Jesus. There is Jesus the Economist, Jesus MD, ET-phone-home-Jesus, Houdini-Jesus, the Great Therapist in the Sky Jesus, and the unforgettable eight pound, six ounce Will Ferrell baby Jesus; just to name a few. With so many versions of Jesus, it is understandable why the identity of Jesus is vague, lost, confused, misrepresented, or abused by so many.

So who is this Jesus that we are supposed to **STAND** up and follow as disciples?

The Bible tells us a lot about Jesus and what He is truly like. We'll highlight a little of who Jesus is here; as we do, we'll include a bunch of verses for you to find in your Bible to help in your own discovering of who Jesus is.

1. JESUS WAS FORETOLD IN HISTORY.
Centuries before Jesus was born, His story was already being told and proclaimed by men of God who prophesied. It is remarkable to see the person and work of Jesus spoken about long before Jesus actually walked the earth as a man.

• Micah 5:2 • Isaiah 7:14 • Zechariah 9:9
• Isaiah 53:4-9 • John 5:39-40

2. JESUS LIVED IN HISTORY.
In fact, even before history began, the Bible tells us that Jesus was there at the point of creation, active with God the Father in creating the universe. Not only that, Jesus entered into human history as a baby, lived and breathed among humankind, and had more influence on history than any other person ever has or ever will. In a section further on, we'll talk more about His life on earth. Until then, check out these Bible verses.

• Colossians 1:15-20 • John 1:1-14 • Luke 2

3. JESUS HAS POWER OVER NATURE.
Because Jesus was part of creating land and sea, monkeys and lions, as well as you and me, Jesus has control over nature. And while He loves us so much that He has given us free

choice to do as we wish, His power over nature and creation is real. Not only did He do crazy things like calm storms, He healed people with incurable diseases, made the blind to see, and even raised the dead to life! Check this out:

• Luke 8:22-25 • Mark 1:30-34 • John 11:1-44

4. JESUS HAS POWER OVER THE SUPERNATURAL.

Again and again throughout the Gospels we see stories of Jesus having power and rule over the supernatural. He had the power to do this then and He still holds the power to do this now.

• Mark 1:22-27 • Mark 3:20-30

5. JESUS HAS POWER OVER DEATH.

Just as Jesus had the power to bring His friend Lazarus back to life from death, He Himself had the power to overcome death. Jesus was brutally murdered by public execution on a cross and, after being confirmed to be dead and buried for three days, Jesus returned to life.

• Mark 15-16 • 1 Corinthians 15:1-8 • Luke 24:1-6

6. JESUS FORGIVES SINS AND BRINGS SALVATION.

All human beings, of every race and rank, of every creed and culture, the moral and the immoral, religious and irreligious, left-handed, right-handed, male, female, hip-hopper and indie rocker, are, without exception, guilty and speechless before God. We have all sinned and fallen short of the perfection and holiness of God. This is the terrible human predicament that we find ourselves in, that everyone everywhere is sinful and separated from God. **In John 14:6, Jesus empathically says, "I am the way, the truth, and the life. No one comes to the Father except through Me."**

• Matthew 9:2-8 • Romans 3:23 • Romans 6:23 • Romans 5:28
• Romans 5:1 • Romans 8:1 • Romans 8:38-39

As you have read through these Scripture references you might have picked out that Jesus is described as both God and man. Sometimes He is God, but other times He was a man with skin and a beard. He probably had stinky feet from walking around so much. How is it possible that He could have been both God and man?

A word that a lot of Christians like to throw around is the term, "incarnation." Incarnation is a fancy theological word that describes how Jesus could be both God and human. The incarnation is what you get when you put God in a skin-suit; Jesus is God in human flesh, God not only taking on human form, but actually becoming human.

That Jesus would leave all the privileges and glory of heaven and being God in order to live as a poor and marginalized man is almost beyond belief. This might be a little bit like Brad Pitt taking on the form of a cat to save the cats.

As you know, cats are generally evil. Like people, they're sinful, moody, and disobedient, they run away, and all they do is eat, sleep and ignore you. They prefer to work in the dark and any chance they get to jump on you in the morning with their claws out, they will. Sheer evil.

If Brad Pitt loved the cats so much that he became a cat in order to reach the cats, he'd have to go through an incredibly humbling experience. He'd have to give up all his fame, wealth, and everything he has in order to become a cat. Sure, he'd start out as a cute and cuddly little kitten, but to live among them and be one would be horrible. In a way, this is what Jesus did. Taking on the very nature of humankind and leaving all of his fame, glory, and prestige, He humbled himself and became a man. Why?

Because He loves us.

The fact that Jesus loves us and was both God and man

is one of the foundational truths of Christianity. Though it is very difficult to believe and impossible to understand how this could be, we're asked to **STAND** up and believe that it is true. In fact, Christianity is held together by the person and work of Jesus Christ. While many religions are held together by a place, a nation, a mosque, a synagogue, a language, a culture, or a period of history, Christianity is held together by Jesus Christ, the God-man.

In the Bible verses above, we've given a brief profile of Jesus as God. But how human was He? Did He really live a life like ours? Was He really human?

Yes, Jesus did live on earth as a man. He would have been a normal looking guy from the ancient Middle East which means, probably, that He didn't look anything like most paintings you've seen of Him. Instead of a tall, good-looking guy with blonde hair, blue eyes, a square cut jaw and rugged European features, Jesus would have been a typical, shorter, Middle Eastern man of his time. Dark hair and eyes would have been the norm and Jewish tradition meant that Jesus was probably rocking a beard.

Yet, regardless of all our speculation, we don't really know what Jesus looked like except that in **Isaiah 53:2** we are told that **"he had no beauty or majesty to attract us to him; nothing in his appearance that we should desire him."** Simply, we don't know what He looked like. He might have had long-flowing hair or He might have been bald and beautiful.

We do know, however, that Jesus was a carpenter, or possibly a stone mason, and that He walked a lot. We know He was a man who did normal manly things: He ate, He drank, He worked a job, He had friends and parents, and He had responsibilities like every man deals with. We also know from the book of Hebrews and three of the Gospels that Jesus was tempted in all the same ways that we are tempted. Wow! Think about that one for a moment.

The big difference? Jesus ate and drank and did all of these normal manly human things and was even severely tempted by Satan himself, without ever sinning. And though He lived without sin; He looked normal and He lived a normal human life.

As a baby He cried and had to learn how to use the potty, whatever that was then. Jesus was a toddler who probably climbed everything He possibly could which meant that he also bumped His big toddler head, just like toddlers do today. Jesus was a teenager who had a mom and dad He had to obey, respect, and listen to, all the while navigating the awkwardness of voice changes, hair in strange places, and having to grow His first Movember moustache. For Jesus, being human meant growing up in a family with brothers and sisters and around a community of other people. Jesus was human.

Jesus was totally normal; He lived a normal human life but He did it all without any sin.

Living a sinful life, actually, was one of the big accusations against the validity of Jesus' claims about himself. Jesus had a lot of critics who insisted that He wasn't sinless. As we read about Jesus, we keep running into these stories of Jesus going to parties, being invited to parties, and doing life with a lot of people that were considered unholy, sinful, and not very clean. He was a friend of drunks and prostitutes and gluttons and the religious elite of His time didn't like this. The thought was that if Jesus hung out with these sinners, obviously He was too.

Nothing could be further from the truth! Yes, Jesus did love food and celebrating at parties and He often did it with people who were far from God. While the temptations to eat too much, drink too much, and sing bad karaoke at parties is a reality, like Jesus we can

STAND in those places without becoming unholy or in some way unclean. That said, if you do **STAND** there, some religious people might not like you either.

Anyhow, the point is that Jesus was God in the flesh and He lived a completely human life, facing all of the normal things that we face during the course of our lifetimes. The real Jesus from the Scriptures is our model and example of how to take a **STAND.** Like Jesus, we face pressures, weird relationships and awkward situations where we are forced to make decisions about how to live and who we are living for. Every single day we make choices about **STANDING** as Christians in a culture that stands for anything else other than Jesus.

This is one of the key points of discipleship: faithfully **STANDING** up, **STANDING** out, and **STANDING** for Christ in a culture that would rather have you sit down, shut-up, and forget about living anything like Jesus. Will you **STAND?**

Jesus **STOOD** when he was hungry, He **STOOD** when people spread horrible rumours about Him, and He **STOOD** when He was dragged into court on jacked-up and false charges. Jesus even **STOOD** while being beaten down and punched in the face before being publicly executed in front of His own mother. Oh, and it was only His mother and a few other women who saw his execution because all of His friends deserted Him.

STANDING for anything isn't particularly easy and **STANDING** for the cause and mission of Jesus is even harder. Thankfully, Jesus becoming flesh and blood does not mean that Jesus ceased to be God. Jesus, even during his time on earth, was still God. In fact, one of the names given to him was Emmanuel, which means, **"God with us."**
Read that again: Jesus is God with us.

Jesus is God with us—**STANDING** beside us, **STANDING** with us, and **STANDING** for us as we live in a world that stands for nothing.

Our God comes into human history and gets His hands bloody, lives a full human life with a full range of human emotions, and suffers and dies. What an amazing story, a great reality! And why? Because Jesus is God and He desperately loves you.

He knows how you hurt, your brokenness, your dying, your failing, your struggling, your loneliness, your abandonment, because He has **STOOD** where you are now.

Will you **STAND** with Him?

» How do I follow Jesus and still be totally into fashion?

» How do I follow Jesus and still play rock and roll in my band?

» How do I follow Jesus and still get ahead in my job?

» How do I follow Jesus and still be involved in the world and culture that I'm from?

These questions are asked over and over again by thousands and thousands of Christians, all trying to figure out how to be faithful and still live in the world that surrounds them. The answer takes all of our searching.

How do Christians engage with culture? When it comes to engaging with culture, where do Christians **STAND**?

Christians, culture, and morality have continually clashed on everything from vegetarianism to alcohol consumption to gay pride parades to the kind of music that should be used for worship. When it comes to living out our faith in a culture that is dark and often twisted, how do we Christians remain true to Jesus while living side-by-side with friends, classmates, and neighbours who could care less about Him?

Thankfully, Jesus gives us some hints as to how to answer this question. Flip open your Bible and take a read of Jesus' prayer in **John 17:1-26**. It's a long prayer but it's awesome. When you get to it, focus on verses 15-18.

Jesus, knowing that He was about to be arrested, knew that His followers were going to have figure out how to live within a culture full of tricky moral issues. What's cool here is that He doesn't give a black and white list of right and wrong; rather, He prays that we'd be sanctified.

Sanctified is a ten-dollar word that means "becoming more like Jesus." When you and I are being sanctified, we are in the process of looking, acting, thinking, and becoming more like Jesus. While some people would have preferred if Jesus had simply made a list of rules and regulations, the heart of this prayer is that we would become more like Jesus. He wanted us to be His disciples.

Unfortunately, too many people mess it up and instead of becoming more like Jesus, they become more like one of two things: (1) A judge and jury, or (2) A hip-hop video.

"GOING TO CHURCH DOESN'T MAKE YOU A CHRISTIAN, JUST LIKE BEING IN A GARAGE DOESN'T MAKE YOU A CAR."

Judge and Jury people believe that if they just followed a long list of rules and regulations without ever messing it up, they'll somehow be good disciples. Often, the thought is this: "If I really want to be a faithful Christian, I have to separate myself from culture completely." In the attempt to **STAND** for Christ in culture, they actually step **OUT** of the culture. Instead of **STANDING** for Christ within culture, what Judge and Jury Christians are actually standing for are their own rules. These oppose culture and make no sense to the people they should be reaching. Judge and Jury folks also like to make judgements about others: what activities, music, movies, and books are appropriate and what kind of people you should or should not hang out with.

Jesus, in fact, prayed against this. He prayed that His followers would not leave the world, disassociate from it, or disengage from culture and, I don't know about you, I don't want to be a part of anything that Jesus prayed against.

"MY OWN PERSONAL JESUS. YO."

On the other side of things, check out the Hip-Hop Video people. You know them: at the award shows they thank God and claim to follow Jesus but when they hit the stage they don't look or sound anything like Jesus. These types of people have become so influenced by the culture around them that they look and act more like culture than Jesus. Sadly, instead of **STANDING** for Christ within culture, these people aren't really **STANDING** for much of anything.

These Hip-Hop Video people look at rules and laws—even the ones that are in the Bible—and think, "Nah, not for me: that's a thing of the past." They usually trumpet grace, calling themselves Christians, believing that God will forgive them. They spend Saturday night getting drunk, disrespecting women, and just generally being morons.

Is this what a disciple looks like? No, not at all. In fact, Jesus prayed against this kind of thinking influencing his disciples: "I pray Father that you would protect them from the evil one." Here, Jesus is praying that we would not become so involved in culture that we forget who we serve.

Which brings us back to the question: "How do Christians **STAND** in culture?" Simply, Jesus is telling us not to leave the world and, at the same time, not to be just like the world.

So what do we do? How do disciples of Jesus be in the world but not of the world?

When I (Ben) was in high school, I was convinced by some buddies to attend my school's fall dance. In the church where I grew up, dancing was about the worst sin you could commit, other than wearing blue jeans to church on Sunday morning. My Dad was the pastor but was not cut from the same legalistic cloth. He knew I wanted to attend the dance and he told me that I needed to start making decisions in my own walk with God. Sheepishly and nervously, I decided to go. Needless to say, when I got there it was more ridiculous and awkward than it was evil. Really, it was a pretty harmless environment overall. While I was at the dance however, my sense was that God had so much more for me than what I thought I might benefit from by trying to be popular, fit in, and impress girls. I didn't stay too long. After talking to a few people and watching a few goofy kids try to impress some girls by doing MJ's trademark moonwalk, I went home. (Okay, I was the goofy kid doing the moonwalk.)

Trying to figure out how to be in the world, but not of the world, is kind of like your first high school dance: it's awkward, nobody really knows what to do, and there are a lot of lights, feelings, and messages all trying to get your attention.

While Jesus walked the earth, He had a close friend named Peter. Peter was a man who travelled with Jesus, heard His teaching first hand, saw Jesus killed and then raised to life again, and even wrote a couple books of the Bible. He was, in many ways, a bit of a spiritual big-shot and many Christians looked up to him. But even Peter had a difficult time answering the question and at one point along the way, he got it totally wrong. He struggled with the question of how to **STAND** in culture.

Thankfully, as the years progressed and as Peter sorted out this question for himself, he offers some instruction on how to live. He said this:

Therefore, with minds that are alert and fully sober, set your hope on the grace to be brought to you when Jesus Christ is revealed at his coming. As obedient children, do not conform to the evil desires you had when you lived in ignorance. But just as he who called you is holy, so be holy in all you do; for it is written: **"Be holy, because I am holy." (1 Peter 1:13-16)**

If you want to **STAND** in culture, being in the world but not of the world, you need to live a holy life. As Christians, we are to be holy like God is holy.

What?! How is that possible? What does it even mean that God is holy?

Holy is the way God is. More than 200 times in Scripture, holiness is seen as an attribute of God or is listed as part of His name. For God to be holy it means that there is no darkness, no impurity, and no evil found in Him. Perfection is who He is.

This also means that everything He does is fully, totally, 100% just, right, and good. He is the standard of what is good and holy. There is no sin, no darkness, and no corruption found in Him.

So when we say that God is holy, we are saying that He is without blemish, mistake, wrong motive, ill-intent, and that He is always 100% good. Not only that, God hates everything (not everyone!) that falls short of being good, whole, or holy.

Unfortunately, when people think about God as holy, they often believe some pretty messed up and wacky stories about Him. This topic of God's holiness has a couple of popular false and damaging narratives that make God out be either an angry judge with a club or a push-over wimp who doesn't care about anything. Both views about God are wrong.

FALSE NARRATIVE #1: GOD IS ANGRY

This narrative is particularly common among people that have grown up in legalistic churches where the fear of God and their pastors' strong rebuke was a very real threat. These are the Judge and Jury Christians who secretly believe that God is out to get them and everyone else.

The angry god of this narrative must be appeased and coaxed into forgiving even the most minor of infractions. There is a lot of guilt and shame attached to this view of God, a God who likes to throw down the divine hammer of judgement and slap you in the face with an "I told you so."

There are too many stories of young people who live under the tyranny and fear of this view of God. They're afraid that God is going to get them with a thunderbolt, cancer, or make them rot in some dark, damp prison somewhere—hell, maybe—if they don't shape up, live right, and avoid screwing up.

There are too many stories of pastors and churches that act as mini-gods dictating what people can and cannot do. Heaven forbid some poor soul enter the church with a hat on, accidentally curse, or in some way mess up; not only is God angry at them, the church is too. This freaks me out.

That's not the God we serve.

When people believe that God is glaring at them and plotting a punishment for them, they begin to fear Him in a way that just isn't healthy. The fear of an angry God and His angry church forces a lot of people into a type of compliance that only serves God so he doesn't squash them. Or so their church friends don't squash them. This destroys any real relationship with God. Instead of being real and open and honest with God and with His community, the church, we are forced to hide who we really are.

What this means is that rather than being able to openly confess sin, repent, and grow, the fear of an angry God with a stick forces people to hide and bury their sin. When this happens, they never deal with the sin and it wreaks havoc on their life.

Simply, the angry God narrative builds legalistic churches and legalistic churches kill Christians.

This view of an angry God turns God's holy indignation into unrighteous sinful human behaviour corrupted by evil and selfish desires. We cannot hold such a view because it would mean that God, like man, needs a saviour to save Him from His own sinfulness. God is holy, perfect, and without sin, meaning that He provides a Saviour, Jesus, and does not need one for Himself.

FALSE NARRATIVE #2: GOD DOESN'T CARE

In this narrative, people tend to ignore any suggestion that God would distinguish between right and wrong. They say that God is so loving and full of grace that He wouldn't judge our actions. This is also a false and damaging narrative. It makes God out to be apathetic, that He doesn't care.

This narrative makes God out to be a tolerant, all-accepting pushover who doesn't really stand for much; a hippie-ish God smoking some weed, accepting all views, opinions, and lifestyles. He condemns nothing and takes a neutral position on everything. This God is one part Mr. Rogers, one part kitten, and one part flower-power. Many people like this God because they do not like authority, responsibility, judgment, or accountability.

I see this all the time with young adults. "Oh yeah, I know it's wrong, but God will forgive me." One young guy who thought this way quoted me a poem:

Sex is sin
God forgives sin
So sex is in.

I'll tell you why this narrative is false: It's false because God is love. Because God loves you so much, He hates the things that will destroy you. Sin is thought and action void of pure love. Sin destroys your relationship with God, it destroys your relationship with yourself, and it destroys your relationship with the world and people around you.

In this narrative of a God who doesn't care, Jesus is no longer the central message of the Bible or even needed at all. If God doesn't judge or even care, then nobody is held accountable and nobody needs a saviour. Nice isn't it?

But do you really want to serve a God who doesn't care and doesn't judge? Do you really want a God who doesn't make a distinction between right and wrong? Would you really want to serve a God who didn't care about rape or genocide? Would you really want to serve a God who just shrugged

His shoulders at child abuse? Would you really want to serve a God who just didn't care about the pain and heartache you feel? Is this really a God worth serving? No, it isn't.

You see, God is holy which means that He is totally for you and totally against the things that are destroying you. Despite our ongoing story of screw-ups and mess-ups, He still loves us. All human beings of every race and rank, of every creed and culture, the religious and irreligious, the well-behaved and the ill-behaved, male, female, hip-hopper and indie rocker, we are all guilty, inexcusable, and speechless before God. There is nobody who is holy.

Yet Peter says, **"Be holy because God is holy."** How? It seems impossible, doesn't it?

All of us know from our own experience that when we became Christians there were still areas in our life where we sometimes fall into sin. Paul felt this struggle too, as he wrote in **Romans 7:21-25—**

So I find this law at work: Although I want to do good, evil is right there with me. For in my inner being I delight in God's law; but I see another law at work in me, waging war against the law of my mind and making me a prisoner of the law of sin at work within me. What a wretched man I am! Who will rescue me from this body that is subject to death? Thanks be to God, who delivers me through Jesus Christ our Lord!

We're not perfect. We're not 100 per cent good all the time. We're not altogether just in our motives. We still tell lies and "half-truths" from time to time. We still find ourselves tempted and sometimes we sin. We know that we're not perfect and we know by our own experience that we're not holy.

Yet the command is, **"Be holy."** It's not try to be holy or give it your best shot at being holy or do everything you can to be holy; it is **"Be holy."** At first glance it seems impossible to really truly be holy. And you're right, without the holy God who is totally for you, and totally against the things that destroy you, holiness is impossible.

One of things we learn about God's holiness throughout the Old Testament is not only that God is holy, but wherever God is that place is holy too. So if God showed up on a mountain, that mountain was suddenly holy. Because God resided in the Temple, the Temple was holy. There is a story of God showing up in a burning bush and even the ground around that bush God becomes holy. Wherever God is, that place becomes holy.

This is huge and significant because as Christians, God the Holy Spirit comes and takes up residence in our lives and guess what, wherever God is, that place becomes holy. And imagine if that place is you—God makes you, and declares you, holy.

Screw-ups and all.

But it doesn't end there. Even though God the Holy Spirit has come and taken up residence in your life and made you holy, the Holy Spirit inside of you is also in the process of making you holy. Remember that ten-dollar word, sanctification? Sanctification is the process of becoming more and more like Jesus (a.k.a. holy) and the job of the Holy Spirit in your life is to do this. The work of God the Holy Spirit living inside of Christians is to shape us and form us to become more like God, holy.

So try to wrap your mind around this: you are holy and at the same time, you are being made holy; screw-ups and all. If God who is in you is holy and is at the same time making you holy, wherever you go God's intention is to make that place holy too. This means that the relationships you have and the places you hang out in are on the edge of becoming holy themselves because God is in you.

This is how we stand in culture. God has placed us there and because He is holy, shaping, and transforming us, the culture and relationships around us transform as well. If you've been changed and are changing, the world around you changes too. If you're scared of culture and in some way afraid of being defiled by it, the world will never be transformed. In the same way, if you become so engaged with culture and are shaped more by culture than you are by the Holy Spirit, the world will never be transformed.

God is holy. God has called you holy. God is making you holy. And He wants to do the same in the world around you.

STAND
IN MISSION

» One of the most remarkable elements of following Jesus is that Jesus asks us to follow Him into the dark, dirty, and twisted places of culture. Yet this Jesus we **STAND** for and who is making us holy gives us this command, **"As the Father has sent me, I am sending you."**

As followers and disciples of Jesus, one of the most significant ways we follow Jesus is to follow Him into mission. I (Jeremy) have given my life to following Jesus in mission and currently find myself living and serving as a missionary in Whistler. Whistler is a crazy and strange little town that would like very little to do with the Gospel. If you've never been to Whistler, it is like a mix between Disneyland, Las Vegas, and Santa's Workshop. It's a town where we can't just hang a church sign, open the doors, and invite people to a church service. Mission and ministry in Whistler require creative, risky, and imaginative forms of mission that we're still figuring out.

Whistler is a town full of artists, designers, mountain people, Europeans, and people living on the fringes of society and culture. It is this eclectic mix of people that has pushed Whistler into the forefront of Canadian culture-making. In fact, Whistler is designated as one of the cultural capitals of Canada, which means what is happening and being tried out in Whistler now will eventually come to your city or town.

Whistler has a reputation for being a party town. The Huffington Post rated Whistler as one of the top five cities in the world to get your party on. I'm okay with this because Jesus had a bit of a reputation of hanging around at parties. In fact, one of the accusations that the Judge and Jury religious folks of Jesus' day made against Him was that He was a glutton and a drunk. Of course, He was neither, but He found Himself hanging around with a crowd that was.

This is who Jesus has sent us to.

Like missionaries who go to China, Africa, and South America, one of my roles as a missionary is in raising funds to finance life and mission in Whistler. This is a long, slow, and faith-inducing process but it allows us to tell stories of what God is doing in Whistler, speak of the vision God has set before us, and invite people into this mission.

In one of these fundraising conversations with a mature and dedicated Christian they told me this: "I would never support a missionary in Whistler because Jesus would never go to Whistler. Jesus wouldn't go to Whistler because God doesn't approve of the culture there."

What?! Jesus wouldn't go to Whistler? Really? I guess Jesus only goes to places, regions, and people that are already holy? I guess it's not the sick who need a doctor, is it? Maybe the whole "For God so loved the world," thing should be re-written to exclude people that Jesus apparently doesn't like.

Now I do understand that not everyone will appreciate that the Gospel actually is light in dark places and some people refuse to believe that Jesus lived in the mud, dirt, and grime of humanity; but the truth is that wherever Jesus went, redemption and restoration followed.

If redemption and restoration follow wherever Jesus is, we should follow Him there too. Just like Jesus was sent into the world, we have been sent to bring restoration and redemption to people and places by the power of the Holy Spirit alive in us. Just like Jesus was sent into the world, His people, the church, are sent as well.

Being sent is an important theme that weaves its way throughout Scripture and really comes to light in the Gospel of John. John deals primarily with the mission of Jesus, from its early origins to the sacrifice of the cross. God the Father sent Jesus and Jesus in turn sent out His disciples, powered by the Holy Spirit.

We are sent. We're sent to places like Whistler and other strange and exotic places like your high school, your part-time job, and your chess club. Yes, Jesus even loves chess players.

One of the most interesting and intriguing little verses in the Bible is found in **Acts 1:1**. To set this up for you, the book of Acts was the second book written by a doctor named Luke. His first volume of work is found in the Gospels.

In his first book, Luke wrote about the life, story, and ministry of Jesus. In **Luke 4:18-19**, he recorded Jesus giving a basic outline of what His life and ministry would look like. Jesus pulled out the Old Testament book of Isaiah and said:

The Spirit of the Lord is on me, because he has anointed me to preach good news to the poor. He has sent me to proclaim freedom for the prisoners and recovery of sight to the blind, to release the oppressed, and to proclaim the year of the Lord's favour.

This is the story Luke chronicled. It's the story of Jesus preaching and speaking about the Kingdom of God; He tells stories, He loves people, large crowds follow Him, people are healed, the oppressed are set free, and the favour of God is evident.

Now back to **Acts 1:1**, which goes like this: **"In my former book, Theophilus, I wrote about all that Jesus began to do and teach."** Let's pause here and break this down into a few short little points:

1. "IN MY FORMER BOOK":
Luke starts out the book of Acts by referring to the last book he wrote, which we know as the Gospel of Luke. In Luke, we see stories of Jesus healing people, feeding people, telling stories, and doing miraculous deeds by the power of

the Holy Spirit at work within His life. The book of Luke was part one of the story and the book of Acts is part two.

2. "THEOPHILUS":

Theophilus is the name of the man who, in all likelihood, funded the writing of the book of Acts. This book of Acts would have been originally written to inform Theophilus of who Jesus was and what His church was like.

3. "I WROTE ABOUT ALL THAT JESUS BEGAN TO DO AND TEACH":

Here, we see that the first book was about what Jesus began to do and teach and the assumption is that now, the book of Acts, is about what Jesus is continuing to do and teach. Acts is part two of the continuing story of what Jesus did.

Here is where it gets interesting: After Acts chapter 1, Jesus isn't in the book any more. He is referred to a number of times but, as odd as it seems, Jesus doesn't really make an appearance. This leaves me to wonder, how does Luke write an entire book about the continuation of what Jesus began to do and teach when Jesus isn't even there? How can he write about the story of Jesus when Jesus is a no-show? What's the deal with that?

The life, story, and ministry of Jesus that began in the Gospel of Luke is an absolutely amazing story of healing, freedom for the oppressed, food for the hungry, sight for the blind, and stories of the Kingdom of God as the Good News is preached. In the book of Acts, the life, story, and ministry of Jesus continues through the life, story, and ministry of the church and its own amazing story! The continuing story of Jesus is lived out through you and I, the church, and is meant to be an ongoing and life-giving story for our world to grasp.

It is a story of mission and of being sent into neighbourhoods, high schools, and homes as well as places far away. Wherever the Gospel has not been heard and wherever Jesus is not known, this is where Jesus is sending us to continue His story.

Think about that for a moment. It is such an honour that we would be called and sent into the same mission that Jesus was sent into—to reach the world with the Good News of the Kingdom of God.

STANDING in mission is not for the faint of heart. Being a continuation of the story of Jesus brings trouble, persecution, and harassment. Living for the cause of the Gospel takes a tremendous amount of courage, particularly when the places you are standing in are dark, grimy, and want nothing to do with the Gospel. Yet here we are, Christians sent on mission and, with the aid of the Holy Spirit, standing in dark places courageously shinning the light. Will you **STAND** in mission?

REFLECTION
Where is your mission?

_____

_____

_____

_____

Who are the people God has sent you to be a missionary to? List some of them by name and take time to pray for them regularly:

_____

_____

_____

_____

_____

_____

STAND
IN THE POWER
OF THE HOLY SPIRIT

» No matter how much you may want to, you can't take a **STAND** in your own strength and Jesus never expected you to do so. In Acts, Jesus told His disciples to go to Jerusalem and wait for the promise. During a special festival called Pentecost, the Holy Spirit filled the room they were gathered in. The sound of wind blew through the room, flames of fire appeared on people's heads, and they all began to speak in languages that they did not know, as God enabled them to do.

The Holy Spirit infused them with the supernatural boldness and dynamite power that Jesus promised they would receive. Peter, one of Jesus' disciples, stood up and preached a message. Thousands of people began to repent and were saved, and miracles took place. From that day forward the disciples of Jesus had great boldness to **STAND,** and in the power of the Holy Spirit, every day people got saved and accomplished crazy, supernatural things that they simply could not have done on their own.

Growing up, attending Pentecostal youth events, I (Ben) heard a lot about the Holy Spirit. I remember one guest speaker at a youth convention in Saskatchewan talking about how the Holy Spirit would give us boldness, so that we could live our lives "Sold out and radical" for Jesus. The thing that stuck out to me was that I could see the speaker's own sincere boldness, love and power. There was something more than his slick sermon and funny jokes that got my attention. I truly saw a supernatural power, grace and a loving boldness flowing through him when he preached and especially when he hung out with us after the service.

As much as I wanted to live sold out and radical for Jesus too, most of the time I found myself feeling insecure, ashamed, and a bit confused in my faith. I knew that I needed everything God had for me and I knew I needed power in my life.

After that youth convention, I attended another church event where they were talking about the Holy Spirit. That night, there was a call to come for prayer for those wanting the baptism of the Holy Spirit, so I went forward. The eager guy on the prayer team seemed nice enough, but he also struck me as a bit odd. Besides his "God's Gym" t-shirt, the strangest thing to me was that he was trying to make me say certain words out loud repetitively, encouraging me to "speak in tongues," as he shouted loudly and put his hands on my mullet. Although I believe this prayer team member might have actually had good intentions, the whole experience felt forced and awkward. I couldn't for the life of me figure out how repeating words and syllables to "speak in tongues" could have anything to do with receiving power in my life. But I wanted to live sold out and radical for Jesus, so I went with it. After a while it was getting too strange, so I left the church meeting that night feeling discouraged and put-off.

Despite that experience, I still felt hungry and sought God for this Holy Spirit power in my life. If God had something for me, I wanted it. One afternoon, no one was home so I decided to go into my room, put on some worship tunes, and read my Bible. As I spent some time just reading and worshiping, I muttered up a prayer: "God, I want everything You have for me. I don't want something forced or fake, I just want You. I know I need supernatural power in my life and I ask You to baptize me with Your Holy Spirit."

I waited a while and listened to a few more songs then the most incredible thing happened to me. It didn't happen right away, but the longer I waited in prayer and worship, the more I felt an incredible and undeniable presence in my room. It felt kind of like a blanket of love, strength and goodness. Was this the power? Was this the Holy Spirit? That afternoon, I know I was baptized in the Holy Spirit. How do I know? Because from that day on I felt a noticeable difference. I felt stronger, bolder and more confident in taking a stand for Jesus. God made Himself real to me in a way that was indisputable.

I talked more about Jesus with my friends at school, I read my Bible more, and I felt strength in my life over the areas of fear and temptation that had left me powerless before. That day, I also began to speak in a supernatural language when I would spend time in prayer. It was only a few phrases that seemed to come to the tip of my tongue at first. As they did, I would spit them out in faith. It wasn't English, but as I spoke them out, I felt strength rising inside of me as the Holy Spirit began to enable me. Sometimes we don't even know what to pray, or how to pray, because we feel things so deeply, but the Bible says in **Romans 8:26** that the Holy Spirit helps us—**"In the same way, the Spirit helps us in our weakness. We do not know what we ought to pray for, but the Spirit himself intercedes for us with groans that words cannot express."**

When I first became a Christian, the Holy Spirit came and lived inside of me. **(Romans 8:9-16; I Corinthians 3:16)** but that was the first day I was baptized, immersed and overflowing with His power in my life. Almost every day since then my prayer has been, "God fill me with Your power today." We need His power every day and the Bible encourages us in **Ephesians 5:18** to **"Keep on being filled with the Spirit."** So every day pray with faith! Expect Him to fill you to overflowing so that His Spirit spills out from your life and splashes onto others. Just like everything else in God's Kingdom, we receive the gift of the baptism of the Holy Spirit in our lives by faith.

Keep seeking the Holy Spirit every day for yourself because I know He will meet you right where you are and give you the power you need, just like He did with me.

DO YOUR OWN STUDY:

Look up these scriptures having to do with both the in-dwelling of the Holy Spirit, and with being filled with the Holy Spirit for witness.

In-dwelling of the Holy Spirit:
• I Cor. 3:16 • 2 Cor. 6:16

Being filled with the Holy Spirit:
• Acts 2:1-13 • Acts 8:14-19 • Acts 9:17-18
• Acts 10:44-46 • Acts 19:1-7

REFLECTION

You can be filled to overflowing with His Holy Spirit even right now. Without His power in your life, you will never be able to truly **STAND!** Take a few minutes to pray. Put down this book, find a quiet place, and ask the Holy Spirit to reveal how He wants to be your friend and helper. Ask Him to fill you with His power so that you can **STAND** for Him in every area of your life. Pray something like this:

Holy Spirit, I want to know You. I'm blown away by Your offer of friendship to me. I want to take You up on Your offer of a lifetime and develop a close relationship with You. I totally desire to partner with You in every area of my life, because I realize that I need You! I want to know You in a personal way, and I want to learn to talk with You. I know that without You it will be impossible to take a **STAND,** but with You I can **STAND** firm! Come fill me and baptize me with Your dynamite power. I want to have Your boldness and Your supernatural power flowing through my life today and every day that I live. Thanks for coming along side of me and giving me the power to **STAND.** In Jesus' name! Amen!

» We are called to **STAND** in faith, but so often our journey is filled with twists and turns and huge uncertainty. Things seem to take longer and often work out differently than expected. We're left scratching our heads and asking, "Where is God in all of this?"

When I (Ben) was ten years old, my grandma sent my sister and me an Easter card with five dollars inside. Grandma's note instructed us to use the money to buy whatever we wanted, so we headed off on our bikes to the mall. Upon arrival, we spotted a pet store and went in, fists full of cash. Now back in the day, pet stores sold things they wouldn't sell today—like baby chickens! We thought this was a great idea so we purchased ourselves two live, baby chicks, jumped on our bikes, and pedaled home as fast as we could with our own two brown lunch bags full of Easter goodness.

Mom almost had a heart attack when she discovered "Heckle and Jeckle," as we decided to call them, but she let us keep them. In fact, Mom warmed up fairly quickly to the idea of two baby chicks as she prepared a hen house for them in the back yard. Mom was pretty excited about the promise of free eggs. I remember her thanking God and telling everyone that God would soon be providing eggs for our family.

The chickens grew quickly and my Mom bought them some steroid-enhanced "laying feed" that was supposed to make the chickens lay super-large eggs. The chickens kept growing, but still, no eggs appeared.

Then it happened.

I remember waking up early in the morning to the most incredible sound coming from outside my bedroom window: "Cock-a-doodle-do! Cock-a-doodle-do!" Heckle and Jeckle were actually roosters. Mom's hopes where completely dashed. She had put all her faith in the fact that these chickens would some day produce eggs for our family.

After our initial shock and disappointment, we decided that Heckle and Jeckle were not worth keeping. The fluffy yellow chicks we had loved so dearly had now become two useless, pent-up, angry birds living in a semi-urban Richmond backyard.

Coincidentally, a farmer from our church randomly told my parents he was looking for some roosters for his hen house. We gladly offered our birds to him, so he came one night and kidnapped them while they were sleeping. He grabbed them by the neck, turned them upside down (they stay asleep apparently), stuffed them in pillow cases and transferred them to his hen house.

What seemed to have been a crisis of faith and major disappointment actually turned out for the good. First, the farmer got some new roosters. Second, that farmer brought two dozen eggs to our front door every Sunday morning, as long as we lived in that house. Third, Heckle and Jeckle woke up that morning in a house full of literal "chicks." Think about it: two dudes, living their whole life together ... They probably thought they had died and gone to rooster heaven.

In **Hebrews 11:1**, we are told that **"Faith is being sure of what we hope for and certain of what we do not see."**

When my sister and I brought home those chicks, my mom began operating in faith. She understood that it would be impossible for baby chicks to produce eggs, but she knew with all her heart that one day they would grow into adult chickens—and everyone knows that adult chickens produce eggs. We never saw the twist coming—the fact that Heckle and Jeckle were actually roosters.

Quite often in your walk of faith, you will find that things don't seem to be working out. Maybe something you've been praying for does not happen. Maybe someone, even God, seems to let you down. You believe in Jesus and His goodness and His promises, but then something happens and you start questioning and doubting. You just can't see how it's going to come together for you. During these times, we need to lean on God's promises like never before. This is when we will need to decide to **STAND** in faith!

My mom was certain that we would one day get eggs. And the great thing is we did. Little did we know that the eggs would come in a such an unexpected way.

I'm too young to have walked the earth with Jesus. I didn't see thousands fed with just a boy's lunch. I've yet to see a man claim to be God and then walk on water. I never got the chance to listen, first hand, to the stories and teachings of Jesus, and I don't fully understand the whole Bible. I never had the opportunity to see the nail holes in the hands of Jesus, or the wound in his side where He was stabbed with a spear during His execution. And no matter how hard I look and how far I search, I don't think I'll ever really clearly see Jesus for who Jesus is, until I finally see Him face-to-face in eternity.

But even though I cannot see Jesus, I have absolute hope and a certainty that He is who He says He is because I see the effects of what He does. I know the impact of His life on me, my family, and my friends. As odd as it seems, though I can't physically see Jesus, I keep seeing Him everywhere I look as my hope and faith rests firmly on the reality that Jesus is God and that He loves each one of us.

This isn't as odd as it sounds. I can't see the wind, but I can see it moving trees, blowing leaves, and powering windmills. How could I possibly say that wind doesn't exist? In the same way, how could I not have faith in Jesus? I've seen God pull me out of addictions, I've seen God pull friends out of car accidents that should have killed them, I've seen God provide food for my family when we were so poor that we couldn't buy milk, and I see the beauty of God's creation every time I go up snowboarding or rock climbing.

He affects everything around us. How could
I say that God does not exist?

In order to **STAND**, we must choose a position of faith. As
Christians, we **STAND** in faith by actively responding to who
God is. In the Bible, we see that as we turn to God and place
our faith in Him, we become more faithful to who He is.

The last twenty-plus winter seasons of my life (Jeremy)
have been spent on a snowboard looking for ways to make
a career out of this silly little sport. In the course of that
time, I've been injured, won contests, been sponsored,
been avalanched, and broken more snowboards and
jumped off more cliffs than most people ever will.

Preparing oneself to jump off a cliff in the mountains is a very
psychologically taxing few moments. It has, at times, flattened
me with a level of anxiety that can only be described as painful.
The uncertainty of what the conditions below are like—snow
stability, hidden rocks or trees, whether or not I'll be able to
control a high speed turn in a narrow run-out—would often
leave me with an almost unbearable apprehension that, even
as I write this, makes my palms sweaty and my heart race.

More recently, though, my pursuits in the mountains have
changed from jumping off cliffs to climbing up them. There are
many inherent dangers in rock climbing and mountaineering to
which even the most cautious are not immune. If you have ever
seen the movie 127 Hours, you'll know that, no matter how
prepared you think you are, the unimaginable can still happen.
Life lived adventuring in the mountains is filled with uncertainty.

My time in the mountains has taught me how to
appreciate the level of discomfort it takes to live with
uncertainty. In fact, no matter where we live our lives,
there are uncertainties and things that we don't know

about that we just have to somehow get over.

Yes, uncertainty can be scary. But without it, it might not be possible to live and experience life with Christ in the real and supernatural way that we desire.

The real problem, I've found, is that certainty simply is not possible. Absolute certainty involves a level of knowledge that belongs only to God. Though there are times when I selfishly and foolishly pretend to be God, I still find myself having to contend with the fact that I do not have full knowledge of the world around me. I simply cannot say, with absolute assurance, that things are true, right, or genuine. I simply don't know; I am uncertain.

Take Jesus, for example. At times, when speaking about Jesus, we project a kind of dressed-up, super-certainty that simply isn't sustainable in the real world. We've trained entire generations of young people to believe that Christ was "simple," "provable," and "obvious," yet when those same young people are faced with the intellect of university or the curiosity of adulthood, they have often found Christ to be anything but.

Instead of raising generations of certainty junkies, we would do better to demonstrate how to live the Christian life with the discomfort of uncertainty. In fact, we might do well to understand that faith does not, and cannot, exist without doubt.

Think of Jesus' disciple, Thomas. Thomas, who history has vilified as "Doubting Thomas," was a courageously loyal man to Jesus **(John 11:16),** eventually put to death by the spear as a missionary martyr in India. This same Thomas, who so famously questioned the other disciples' witness of Jesus' resurrection, later made the bold exclamation of the divinity of Christ, **"My Lord and my God!"**

What I love about Thomas is his courage to doubt, reason, and think through the complexities of his faith, which eventually led him to a run-in with the supernatural. Scripture shows that when Thomas doubted, Jesus showed up! Jesus, instead of rejecting him and banishing him from the disciples, actually honoured his uncertainty by confronting him with the reality of who He is.

Many of us, however, have a tendency to place our faith in things other than God. We place our trust and faith in money, music, fame, or in a relationship with a boyfriend or girlfriend. But whatever our faith stands on, that is what we become faithful to. For example, if you put all of your faith, trust, and security in money, what will eventually happen is that you will begin to faithfully serve money. Money will become your master and you its slave.

So where will you put your faith? What does your faith **STAND** on? My faith **STANDS** on the person and work of Jesus.

I believe in Jesus. I believe He is the Word made flesh, that He is both human and divine, and is God the Father's Son who died at the hands of Roman executors and rose to life three days later. I believe He was present at creation, and will come again to establish His Kingdom and restore all that we've destroyed. I have this great hope that He is who He says He is and I have faith that some day, despite all of my uncertainties, Jesus will look me in the eye and say, **"Well done, good and faithful servant."**

REFLECTION

Before you read any further, take a few moments to prayerfully think about some things you are believing God for and that you are **STANDING** in faith for in your life. Write them down.

Things I'm **STANDING** in faith for in my life:

_____

_____

_____

_____

_____

_____

_____

STAND
IN PRAYER

» For most Canadians the thought of global warming doesn't sound like too big a deal. In fact, a warmer winter and longer summer doesn't sound half bad. Well, not so fast.

Scientists in white lab coats say that the issue of global warming is a real and harmful issue. The experts over at South Park did five episodes on global warming and even Vice President Al Gore got in on the action with the money-making documentary An Inconvenient Truth.

The consensus is that pollution is a real problem and we should be thinking through the effects our actions have on the atmosphere. The atmosphere, a.k.a. "air," allows us to breathe in life while at the same time serves as a shield blocking out harmful ultra-violet radiation from the sun. Without it, we're dead and by destroying it, we're dying. The atmosphere, as it turns out, is very important.

Some estimates show that as many as 4.6 million people die each year from causes directly attributable to air pollution. Worldwide, more deaths per year are linked to air pollution than to car accidents. This is an interesting piece of trivia considering that it is the automobile that creates most of the air pollution! In the end, your busted up old beater car will kill you by serving up some form of aggravated asthma, bronchitis, emphysema, lung and heart disease, and respiratory allergies.

But cars, trucks and those old diesel burning hippie-vans that environmentalists drive aren't the only causes of destruction to our atmosphere. Factories, forest fires, volcanoes, burning any kind of fossil fuel, pine trees, and the methane produced from digested food all contribute to the breakdown of our atmosphere. Did you read that?

Methane produced from digested food. People and animals fart enough to rank as major players contributing to a toxic atmosphere. And though you laugh and joke about how that smelly friend of yours is going to kill you if he eats a burrito, he actually will.

And so the simple story is this: if we keep screwing up the atmosphere it will kill us.

That's why I want to talk about prayer.

Prayer was the atmosphere of the early church. The book of Acts, which records the earliest history of the church, shows us that the first Christians were totally devoted to prayer. The atmosphere of the church and the air that they breathed was prayer. It brought them life, it's what protected them, and it's what the early church knew to be absolutely vital to their faith. Not only that, but this early church, **STANDING** in an atmosphere of prayer, changed the world.

When Christians live within an atmosphere of prayer, the world changes.

But first, what is prayer?

Simply, prayer is communication between us and God. Or to put it another way, we speak to God, and God speaks to us. I love the simplicity of this definition because it reminds me that my relationship with God is personal and real and not about trying to appease some angry old man in the sky. In many ways, communicating to God (although extremely profound that you can actually freely communicate with the God of the universe), is as basic as texting your friends, posting on someone's Facebook page or chatting on Skype.

Our God is a God who wants to speak with us; He wants to speak to us personally in the midst of our smiles, pain, and in every single one of life's circumstances.

Prayer is rugged and beautiful, raw and emotional, sculpted and free-form, and it often comes upon us when we least expect it. Sometimes prayer becomes part of our schedule and our routine while other times it is our natural response to life around us and God within us. More remarkably, if we listen, we find that God is speaking to us all the time. Martin Luther said it this way, "God writes the Gospel, not in the Bible alone, but also on trees, and in the flowers and clouds and stars." God is constantly, and by every means possible, trying to speak with us.

This is the atmosphere in which we Christians must live and when we do, the world changes.

When we hear God speaking to us, we **STAND** up for the hungry.

When we hear God speaking to us, we **STAND** beside the hurting.

When we hear God speaking to us, we **STAND** with the oppressed.

When we hear God speaking to us, we **STAND** as beacons for the lost.

When we hear God speaking to us, we **STAND** under the weight of each other's burdens.

When we hear God speaking to us, we **STAND** and fight for clean drinking water for third world countries.

When we hear God speaking to us, we **STAND** and fight for the rights of women and children sold into slavery.

When we hear God speaking to us, we **STAND** and fight for a world that broken, dysfunctional, and hurting.

When we hear God speaking to us, we **STAND** up and the world changes.

This is why we must live our lives in an atmosphere of prayer and do everything we can to protect and maintain it. Just like the air we breathe, the atmosphere of prayer can become polluted. Here are three common pollutants:

1. BUSYNESS:

Life can be very, very fast and cluttered with so many things to do that prayer often gets pushed to the side, forgotten about, or is only muttered quickly under the breath while consuming that drive-thru hamburger. The busier our lives tend to be the more likely it is that the atmosphere of prayer gets choked out.

2. SELFISHNESS:

Another prayer pollutant happens when our prayer is only about us. "God, please help me ... give me this ... show me how to ..." and the list of me-inspired prayers grows and grows. When prayer becomes primarily about you, it's polluted.

3. MANIPULATION:

Sometimes we pray hoping to manipulate or somehow strong-arm God in to doing what we want. If we pray long enough, hard enough, or beautifully enough, God will have to listen, right? Nope. It just stinks up the atmosphere.

What does **STANDING** in an atmosphere of prayer look like? Well, the Bible urges Christians to continue faithfully in prayer **(Romans 12:12),** to pray always **(Luke 18:1),** to pray continually **(I Thessalonians 5:17),** to pray everywhere **(I Timothy 2:8),** to pray on all occasions with all kinds of prayer **(Ephesians 6:18),** to persevere in prayer **(Colossians 4:2),** to pray humbly **(Matthew 6:5-7),** and to pray powerfully **(James 5:16).**

In Acts, the atmosphere of prayer had some characteristics that showed up over and over again. Even though this doesn't tell us how to pray, it gives us a good picture of what the atmosphere was like.

The early church often prayed together **(Acts 1:14, 2:42, 3:1, 4:24, 4:31, 6:4, 6:6, 8:15, 12:5, 13:3, 14:23, 16:13,16,25, 20:36, and 21:5).**

The early church prayed regularly **(Acts 1:14, 2:42,**

3:1, 6:4, 10:2, 10:9-16, and 16:13,16).

The early church prayed in times of crises **(Acts 4:24, 6:4, 7:59, 9:9-12, 12:5, 16:25, and 20:36).**

The early church prayed for healing, miracles, repentance, and to receive the Holy Spirit **(Acts 1:14, 2:42, 3:6, 4:24-31, 8:15, 8:22, 9:9-12, 9:40, 10:2, 10:9-16, 12:5, and 28:7-10).**

The atmosphere of the early church was prayer. As a generation of young Christians hoping and dreaming to change the world, the call is clear: we have to pray. In **Ephesians 6:18-20,** Paul instructs us to pray, and so we should.

What will you pray?

In **Matthew 6,** Jesus had some great things to say about prayer. We can know that when we do pray, God our Father hears us. He knows what we need and nothing is too hard for Him to handle.

REFLECTION

Take some time and read **Matthew 6:5-14.** Jot down some things that God might show you from the scriptures about prayer. Use the chart below to help you track your prayers. Write down what you are going to **STAND** in prayer for (it could be a person or a situation). When the prayer has been answered, fill in the date in the space provided.

I AM PRAYING FOR:

Date _____

Subject _____

Answer _____

_____

Date

Subject

Answer

Date

Subject

Answer

Date

Subject

Answer

Date

Subject

Answer

Date

Subject

Answer

Date

Subject

Answer

STAND
IN SCRIPTURE

» Many different and competing voices shape what we believe about God. Music, ad campaigns, TV shows, movies, friends, and all kinds of people try to craft what we believe and tell us what we should buy and who we should look like. If we don't know where we **STAND** and what we **STAND** on as followers of Jesus, we'll simply become disciples of culture instead of disciples of Jesus.

To follow Jesus well, disciples need to learn some theology (as boring as that word might seem!). We should be diving deep into Scripture, learning the stories and the character of God and working out what we believe. How we experience God crafts what we believe about Him. We need both to study God and to experience God.

But first, let me give you a quick primer on theology.

Theology is often misunderstood as a long, drawn-out, boring study of an ancient god from an ancient, irrelevant book that only old people with comb overs and tweed jackets do. And though it is entirely possible that more Christians have read the Left Behind series or watched the Narnia movies than have actually read their Bible, it is not accurate to suggest that theology is only for musty-smelling Bible thumpers.

Theology is the study of God. God, in His divine wisdom, has chosen to reveal parts of who He is through His Son, Jesus Christ, and through His written word, the Bible. This means there are aspects of God that we can discover and explore, and other parts that God has chosen to keep hidden, undisclosed, and mysterious. It's this hidden piece that tends to throw people for a loop as they try to figure out exactly who God is. The reality is that God hasn't shown us every part of who He is.

Yet, as we read and re-read our Bibles, we can begin to grasp God's character. The more we learn who God is, the stronger we **STAND.** Scripture in its entirety is God's primary way of communicating with us, revealing His character, attributes, promises, and, ultimately, revealing His Son Jesus Christ.

A very early definition of theology was "union with God through prayer," which, if we're honest with ourselves, sounds pretty out there. Unfortunately for the tie-dyed, long-haired, non-conformist hippie in all of us, union with God actually means submission to His rule and reign. When we come to Scripture, we must come in prayerful submission and repentance, recognizing that the Bible is the authority that we live by. A humble study and application of Scripture should, above all else, point us to God, move us to worship, and energize us towards conforming our lives to look more like the life of Jesus our King and Savior.

Sadly in a culture whose anthem is "Raise your fist, rebel, resist," the question of humble submission to anyone's authority—especially that of the Bible—is openly mocked. Together, as a generation of young followers of Jesus, we will continually be faced with the complicated issue of faithfully **STANDING** in Scripture while honestly living in a culture who would like us to do anything but follow Jesus.

As we follow Jesus, Scripture serves as our guidebook and map to help us discover who Jesus is, how we relate to Him, and it how to live well among our friends, at school, or wherever else we are. The Bible sustains us, it encourages us, it teaches us, it corrects us, and it trains us.

REFLECTION

The next 26 short sections of **STAND** have been contributed by youth pastors and youth workers from across BC and Alberta who love Jesus, are guided by Scripture, and who want to help teenagers follow Jesus. These are meant to be read slowly over the course of maybe a month or so and will be a useful resource for you to return to as you go through the muck and grime of life. Each entry deals with a particular topic and was added here to help show you how to **STAND** in the truth and promises of Scripture. We hope that as you read the Scripture and the devotional thoughts that go with them, you will be inspired to dig deeper into your Bible, discover Scripture, and **STAND** strong in your faith.

DEV. 1 | STAND EVEN WHEN DISCOURAGED

» **"Don't let your hearts be troubled. Trust in God, and trust also in me." John 14:1**

As Jesus looked at His disciples, He knew what was going on in their minds and hearts, how disturbed and upset they were, and what was causing their turmoil. He knew the remedy for their anxieties as well. Many of us suffer from the same affliction as these disciples—circumstances troubling and upsetting us.

Twice in this chapter Jesus gave the directive, **"Do not let your hearts be troubled" (verses 1 and 27).** The second time He added, **"And do not be afraid."** Jesus gives us the responsibility of not allowing our hearts to be troubled or afraid. However He doesn't just leave us floundering, He tells us how to overcome this fear. **"Trust me,"** He says. Sounds simple enough but we soon find it is easier to be troubled than to trust.

When we trust in God, we are not actually trusting God to remove all our difficulties. Rather we are trusting Him to be sustain us in those difficulties. We are trusting God to give us the wisdom and guidance to know what to do in any situation. We are believing that He is in control of all our circumstances.

We would like God to rescue us from our troubles but God has not promised us a life of safety. He has promised us His presence, His grace, and His wisdom. He has also promised never to leave us nor forsake us, and that is enough.

We trust God, not because He is safe or promises us a life of safety, but because He is good. We trust in the character of God, knowing an all-good God will not allow us to be tempted beyond our capacity or tried beyond endurance. He knows what we can bear.

REFLECTION

What have you been discouraged about lately?

_____

_____

_____

_____

What is encouraging about Jesus' words in John 14:1?

_____

_____

_____

_____

Who might you be able to encourage this week with that same promise?

_____

_____

_____

_____

REMEMBER: "Sometimes one of the best ways to overcome personal discouragement is to find someone else to encourage."

DEV. 2 | STAND DESPITE WORRY

» **"Give all your worries and cares to God, for he cares about you." 1 Peter 5:7**

In times when world-changing events are happening all over the place and the future can seem uncertain, it is good for us to remember one of the greatest privileges we have as Christians, as outlined in **1 Peter 5:7—"Casting all your cares upon him, because he cares for you."** In this verse, we are instructed to throw each and every worry and anxiety upon God based upon the fact that He cares for us.

There is much we can learn from tough situations in our lives. We may find ourselves in harsh circumstances that give us great moments of worry. We can feel as if God does not care and begin to panic. But through it all, we must realize that God is not panicked about the situation.

Was Jesus worried in the back of the boat **(Mark 4:35-40)?** Then why should the disciples worry? Then why should you worry? We can rest in the fact that God is in perfect control and is completely capable of removing the storms in our life if He chooses—yet we will still be safe even if He does not. Our problem always boils down to an issue of faith. Are you willing to trust Him? Just as you confidently throw yourself upon your bed after a long day, confidently throw your cares upon Him because He is able to handle them. The times may seem difficult, but we have a great God who can handle all of our worries, and we can live lives of faithful obedience, and not of fearful worry.

Read Mark 4:35-40.

REFLECTION

What storms are going on in your life right now?

_____

_____

_____

_____

Jesus said to the waves and the wind, "Peace, be still." What might Jesus speak over your personal storm?

_____

_____

_____

List some cares and worries that you have been carrying on your own, that you are now asking Jesus to carry for you.

_____

_____

_____

_____

_____

_____

_____

DEV. 3 | STAND WHEN HURT

» **"He heals the broken-hearted and bandages their wounds." Psalm 147:3**

We know God sees everything that happens to us—our hurts, our losses. Nothing is a surprise to Him. We wish He would intervene and stop the pain, but as our lives play out we find ourselves with a choice to make.

We can believe God is a God of love or we can turn from Him in anger.

We can believe that His heart is always for us, or we can believe He is unfair and mean.

Make the right choice. Running to Him in the midst of our hurt will take us into His arms of comfort. Pushing Him away will leave us alone with desperation in our hearts.

In times of severe circumstances and agonizing grief, the hope that we have as Christians is the knowledge that God does care and He will help us through. Often our unanswered questions leave us blaming God and we distance ourselves from the very One who can bring comfort to the brokenhearted.

When we don't understand the twists and turns of our life we can run to the One who will comfort us. He doesn't promise our lives will be free of trouble, yet He does promise to hold us close through it all. Never doubt God's love and care. He hurts when you hurt. His Son, Jesus, went up the agonizing hill to the cross and understands the deep anguish the soul can plunge to. That's why we can trust Him to be with us in our times of overwhelming pain.

REFLECTION

What area do you need personal healing in?

_____

_____

_____

If you were to ask God to heal you right now, what would you say? Use the space below or a separate page to write out a deeply honest prayer to God, asking Him to heal you.

_____

_____

_____

_____

_____

_____

_____

_____

_____

_____

_____

_____

DEV. 4 | STAND WHEN FEELING DOWN

» **"Praise be to the God and Father of Lord Jesus Christ, the Father of compassion and the God of all comfort, who comforts us in all our troubles, so that we can comfort those in any trouble with the comfort we ourselves have received from God." 2 Corinthians 1:3-4**

My mom died when I was thirteen, passing away very suddenly. It was actually my brother and I that found her. There has been no other moment in life that presented me so clearly with two very different options. I had to choose if I was going to have God help me get through this or have the world help me get through this.

I remember being dumped by a girl I was in love with. We had dated for a long time and I had given a lot to be with her. I took it really hard and figured that nothing in my life could possibly be good again. Again, I had to choose if I was going to have God help me get through it or have the world help me get through it.

Over and over again in our lives, we face events and situations that hurt—the loss of a loved one, a broken heart, or some other unique and painful thing. There's no way to avoid hurt and pain in the world we live in. We cannot control it.

We can, however, control how we respond when those hard

times come upon us. Often that choice is between turning to God in our pain or turning to the things of this world.

The things the world prescribes for pain—sex, drinking, drugs, rebellion—offer temporary relief but usually lead to more trouble. What God offers is comfort, compassion, and care **(2 Corinthians 1:3-4).** What God offers is good, righteous, and forever.

To **STAND** as a Christian is to choose God as your comfort rather than the things of the world. When trouble, pain, and hurt come, which will you choose?

REFLECTION

What are some things you have turned to when you've been feeling down? Did they work long term?

_____

_____

_____

_____

Read the story of Elijah **(1 Kings 19:1-12)** when he was feeling discouraged. How did God bring comfort to him during his time of discouragement?

_____

_____

_____

_____

DEV. 5 | STAND OVER GUILT AND SHAME

» **"Therefore, if anyone is in Christ, he is a new creation; the old has gone, the new has come!" 2 Corinthians 5:17**

I went to Bible College with a guy who used to sell a lot of drugs. Through some interesting experiences in prison, he came to know Jesus and made his way to Bible College. When we graduated four years later, he was a completely different man. He will always be, to me, an example of how powerful the grace of God is.

It's really difficult to understand how forgiving God is. No one on earth is as forgiving as Him. Nothing you or I say or do can disqualify us from God's love as long as we genuinely and humbly apologize and try to do better.

So what does that mean for us? Well, Scripture tells us that because of our faith in Christ we are, in God's eyes, a new creation. Nothing in our past—not our mistakes, our bad decisions, the things we regret—counts against us.

You know that thing you feel guilty about? Yeah, that one, the thing that creeps into your mind when you start getting closer to God? I had one of those too; a ball of guilt for something I did which was used to keep me from growing closer to God.

If you've asked Him for forgiveness, when God looks at you He doesn't see it. He doesn't think about it. He doesn't hold against you. That's the thing about God's grace: it makes us new. We can stop letting our regrets and guilt hold us back from growing closer to God. **STANDING** up for Christ when you're feeling guilty means recognizing that God's grace makes you new.

So, if God isn't holding it against you,
why hold it against yourself?

Read Romans 7-8. Memorize 2 Corinthians 5:17 and Romans 8:38.

DEV. 6 | STAND IN THE MIDST OF CONFUSION

» **"If any of you lacks wisdom, he should ask God, who gives generously to all without finding fault, and it will be given to him." James 1:5**

God only ever clearly indicated what He wanted me to do once, when He showed me I was supposed to go to Bible College. I did that thing where you pray that if a specific thing happens, you will take it as God's confirmation that you're supposed to do something. I told him that if I won a bursary I would know I was supposed to go to Bible College. I won. I went.

For the whole rest of my life, though, it hasn't happened like that. It's always kind of like driving in foggy weather. You only see very close in front of you. Signs don't come into your vision until they're just right there. You can kind of tell the curves in the road from the tail lights of the car in front of you. And you can only really tell that you're on the right side of the road by all the cars you see going the other way.

Often, that's how our walk with God is. And if you're feeling kind of like that, well, you're probably doing it right. So I want to encourage you: keep driving forward in the midst of confusion.

Don't worry if you can only see very close in front of you. The signs will come at the right time, even if that moment is immediately before the turn. Watch people in front of you for examples of where you should go and what you should do. And if there are lots of people going in a different direction than you, don't worry—the Christian walk is supposed to be a different direction than the rest of the world.

STANDING for Christ when things are confusing is all about knowing that the God who loves you knows what He's doing. Often people give up and sit down when they don't know what to do.

So, when things are complicated and confusing, will you give up and sit down or stay **STANDING?**

Take some time and ask God for wisdom. He said He would give you the wisdom you need so go for it. Be specific.

REFLECTION

Who is someone you might be able to follow as a godly example? A youth pastor? Leader, friend?

_____

_____

_____

If that person is willing, take the initiative to discuss what a regular discipling or mentoring relationship might look like.

DEV. 7 | STAND AGAINST TEMPTATION

» **"Be alert and of sober mind. Your enemy the devil prowls around like a roaring lion looking for someone to devour. Resist him, standing firm in the faith, because you know that the family of believers throughout the world is undergoing the same kind of sufferings." I Peter 5:8-9**

You've been there before haven't you? Tangled in the crossfire of temptation. Your mind is flustered with rationalizations and conviction, leaving you in a daze of confusion. Temptation is a pull, a lure to capture your heart. Dangling before you, temptation can take on many forms. From stealing to cheating, from sex to binging, the list is endless and individualistic. The whirlwind of temptation can quickly sweep you off your feet all the while feeding your carnal desires, sending you into a tizzy if you allow it to.

How can anyone withstand the appeal and whirling captivation of temptation?

Peter says be alert, and sober-minded. The battle ends where it begins: in your mind and thoughts. Just like a whirlwind can rise up quickly, your thoughts can also quickly spin out of control. It is best to be on guard and clear-headed. If a whirlwind was spinning towards you, you wouldn't run towards it: you would take cover!

If you flirt with the danger, even if only to get a "closer look," you may get swept into its alluring draw. Instead, think clearly and resist it altogether so that you can decipher the truth amidst the flurry of lies. Resist, take cover over your heart, and **STAND** firm in your faith. Choose to resist temptation before its whirlwind consumes you.

1. PRAY
Remember that temptation is not sin. Be honest with God and openly confess areas in your life where you are facing temptation.

2. READ
Think about **1 Corinthians 10:13—"No temptation has seized you except what is common to man. And God is faithful; he will not let you be tempted beyond what you can bear. But when you are tempted, he will also provide a way out so that you can stand up under it."**

3. STRATEGIZE
God has promised He will provide a way out when we are tempted. Visualize the next tempting situation you might find yourself in, then in your mind, plan ahead of time what you will do, what you will say, and how you will be able to find God's way out. Do this several times and you will be amazed at how God will give you the power you need to do what's pleasing to Him.

DEV. 8 | STAND DOWN WHEN ANGRY

» **"In your anger do not sin. Do not let the sun go down while you are still angry, and do not give the devil a foothold." Ephesians 4:26**

Can you remember the last time you were angry—really really angry? Although anger often gets a bad rap, there are times when anger catapults us into fighting for injustice, causing us to seek righteousness. But there are also times when anger has little to do with the betterment of others and more to do with revenge and the self-interest. When someone leaves us feeling cheated, our initial human reaction is to retaliate in anger.

So how do you take a **STAND** when you are angry and ready to lose it? Paul in **Ephesians 4:26** says, **"In your anger do not sin. Do not let the sun go down while you are still angry, and do not give the devil a foothold."**

Paul doesn't say that anger itself is a sin, yet he warns about the dangers of anger. If you stay in the anger zone for too long you run the risk of allowing Satan to gain a base in your life, a base for further advancement. He will feed into your anger, adding fuel to your fire. What may have started as a simple spark can lead to a full blazing fire of sin. Paul offers some advice to fight your way out of the anger. When he says **"do not let the sun go down while you are still angry,"** he is reminding us not to stay angry for too long. For when you meditate on the offence and fuel the fire of anger in your heart, you give Satan a way in. So the next time you are angry, take a close look at your heart.

Take a **STAND** by taking it to God so that you can shut out the devil before he gains a foothold in your life!

Is there someone you've been angry with and you know you need to make things right? Make a plan to talk with them about it as soon as possible. Be the mature one and start the conversation by asking their forgiveness if you did something to offend them.

DEV. 9 | STAND BY YOURSELF

» John 17:20-26

In the book of Daniel, there is a famous story about three teenagers, Shadrach, Meshach, and Abednego, who were captured and forced to live in Babylon, a place obsessed with the occult, magic and idol worship. One day, the king ordered everyone to bow down and worship a statue. Everyone did, except for Shadrach, Meshach, and Abednego, who chose to **STAND** alone. They told the king in **Daniel 3:18, "We want you to know, Your Majesty, that we will not serve your gods or worship the image of gold you have set up."**

These teenagers resolved to take a **STAND** by themselves and live for God in the middle of this dark culture. Even though they were disconnected from their home, their old friends, their old school, and all of the things they were familiar with, they were at their core completely connected to God.

This defiance and willingness to **STAND** alone made the king extremely angry and he ordered them to be burned alive in a giant furnace. The raging king tossed the three guys in the fire, but they did not burn up. The Bible says that they didn't even smell like smoke! Even crazier, the king noticed four figures in the fire walking around unharmed. The extra person that met them in the fire was God Himself.

As you resolve to **STAND** for God, He will always **STAND** with you. It was more than just guts that helped them **STAND** —I believe they stood alone because they were dedicated to God. They knew Him, and His faithfulness, personally.

It is possible to be lonely even when you are in a crowd of people. I bet these Hebrew boys felt alone in Babylon. They couldn't have felt a kinship with others around them because they had a totally different set of values.

There may be days when you feel all alone. No one at school understands, no one at home understands, and there is an empty pit in your stomach. But there is someone who always understands. During His trial, Jesus watched one of His best friends betray him. On the cross, He cried out to His Father, **"Why have you forsaken Me?"**

Jesus understands loneliness—but He also understands connectedness. Jesus was one with His Father, as we read in **John 17:21-22.** In the same way He and the Father are connected, we as Christians are connected to Jesus and one another. As a Christian, you are never truly alone because loneliness comes from being disconnected.

It is true that at times you may feel disconnected from your friends, your classmates, and even your family. Maybe they don't follow Jesus and don't understand why you would want to. You may feel all alone in your faith, but the truth is you are not alone.

Even when you feel like you are **STANDING** in the fire or **STANDING** by yourself, there are more than a billion other people in the world to which you are connected through Jesus. So when you **STAND** against loneliness, remember that you do not **STAND** alone; rather you **STAND** with Christ and with the many people who believe in Jesus, just like you do.

DEV. 10 | STAND AS A RIGHTEOUS REBEL

» **"Your attitude should be the same as that of Christ Jesus: Who, being in very nature God, did not consider equality with God something to be grasped, but made himself nothing, taking the very nature of a servant, being made in human likeness. And being found in appearance as a man, he humbled himself and became obedient to death – even death on a cross!" Philippians 2:5-8**

Think about the coolest person you know. What is it that makes him or her so cool? Is it because they have an air of rebellion about them? Why is it considered cool in our world to rebel; almost as if it is expected, especially among teenagers? People will rebel against many things. They protest and rebel against our society that embraces greed and materialism. They rebel against the church for being too traditional and legalistic. They rebel against authority. What is it that makes being a rebel so appealing?

In a good way, taking a **STAND** is rebelling. When you take a **STAND** against rebellion, you are following the steps of Jesus. In **Philippians 2:5-8,** Paul reminds the church that Jesus took a **STAND** against rebellion, by humbling Himself in obedience to God's will. **John 1:1** says that Jesus is God and has always been God, yet He gave it all up out of obedience to God's will. It was not an easy life that He chose, in fact it led to

His death, but He understood that this was what God wanted.

Rebellion is a natural part of life and has been connected with humankind ever since Adam and Eve rebelled against God and ate the forbidden fruit. Children naturally rebel against their parents, God's creation naturally rebels against Him. It is always easier to rebel than it is to humble ourselves to God and live an obedient life. As Christians, it is important for us to put aside our selfish, self-serving desires and follow the plans that God has made for us.

If you really want to stand out from the crowd and rebel in a positive way, choose a backward way of thinking: humility and obedience to the Father. If you choose to take a **STAND** against rebellion it won't always be easy, but remember that Jesus showed us how it is done and He will walk with us every step of the way.

DEV. 11 | STAND THROUGH REJECTION

» **"The Lord is near to the broken hearted and saves the crushed in spirit." Psalm 34:18**

Rejection is one of the worst experiences that a person can suffer in life, yet it is a common human experience. Have you ever felt the sting of rejection? It takes many forms. A friend won't talk to you because they are mad. A parent tells you to go away because they don't want you around anymore. The more you are rejected, the harder it is to find true relationships.

Rejection can lead you to put up walls so that no one can hurt you again. People often reject others as a defence mechanism because they fear the rejection that might be on its way. The walls around their hearts grow and stretch up higher and higher until they feel as if there is no way out. If you have been trapped within the walls of rejection, there is good news and a way out. Jesus feels your pain, for He understands the feelings of rejection. He came to set the world free from sin and oppression. He gave up His divinity and took on humanity to bring the good news with Him. Yet He was rejected and mocked by the very people He came to save.

Jesus can help you to overcome the wall of hurt and pain. His heart is very close to yours and He wants to help you. He came to bind up the broken hearted and He will **STAND** with you as you take a **STAND** against the rejection in your life. Don't let the pain of rejection keep you locked within its confining fortress, keeping you from finding fulfilling relationships. Let Jesus bring peace and bind up your broken heart, trust in Him, and He will help you **STAND**.

DEV. 12 | STAND IN THE FACE OF FEAR

» **"For God did not give us a spirit of timidity, but a spirit of power, of love and of self-discipline." 2 Timothy 1:7**

Phobophobia is a fancy way to say that someone is afraid of fear. Fear for many of us can usually be reduced to a short list that summarizes the basics: spiders, toenails, heights and darkness. Did you know it has been said that people are more afraid to speak in public then they are of death?

I like what the Bible says about fear. First, it is made clear that fear is a real issue that we all must deal with. Second, it says that fear is not something that we need to be afraid of.

When we face fear head-on, we need to remember that God did not intend for us to live in a spirit of fear but in a spirit of peace and power.

So what are you afraid of? In the Christian life, we need to continue to come back to the place where God wants us to be. To allow Christ to be the person who confronts our fears head on and who brings us the freedom that He desires for each one of us. As you daily release the things that cripple you in fear, are you allowing Christ to transform that fear into freedom? If not, why not start today by giving God your fear and, in turn, receiving the power, love and self-control that is spoken about in God's Word?

DEV. 13 | STAND THROUGH UNCERTAINTY

» **"Without weakening in his faith, he faced the fact that his body was as good as dead—since he was about a hundred years old—and that Sarah's womb was also dead. Yet he did not waver through unbelief regarding the promise of God, but was strengthened in his faith and gave glory to God, being fully persuaded that God had power to do what he had promised." Romans 4:19-21**

Sometimes it's easy to think that we've screwed up too much or missed our chance for God to use us. But if we look at the miracles in the Bible, we see otherwise. Abraham was a man of faith who fell on his face and messed up many times, but through everything, continued to be faithful to God. God then used him in incredible ways. Just when it seemed like his time was up and he wouldn't ever have children, his NINETY-year-old wife gave birth to Isaac **(Genesis 21:1-3).**

Remember, in life there will be things that seem impossible and circumstances that seem unworkable–but with God, all things are possible **(Matthew 19:26).** In the darkest and seemingly impossible times, remember God is still God and He is faithful. We don't always understand, or even know what He is doing or why He is doing it, but remain faithful. Give God the opportunity to show off through your circumstances and bring glory to His name.

Next time you feel like you've messed up too much for God to use you, or feel like nothing good could come of your situation, just remember: remain faithful to God. God's plans are bigger than yours or mine, and God uses flawed people to do incredible things, over and over and over again. As the saying goes, "God does not call the equipped, he equips the called."

God knows you, your situation, your strengths, your weaknesses, and He will use them in incredible ways. All you have to do is trust that God will work through them even when you don't see how that's possible. God brings glory to His name and beauty from brokenness in the most unlikely places. That's why we trust Him and lean not on our own understanding **(Proverbs 3:5).**

DEV. 14 | STAND WITH FAITH

» **"If you can?" said Jesus. "Everything is possible for one who believes." Immediately the boy's father exclaimed, "I do believe; help me overcome my unbelief!" Mark 9:23-24**

The desperate father asked Jesus to heal his demon-possessed boy if He could. How often do we come to God with a half-hearted belief that He can do something? A prayer that we hope He'll answer. Jesus seemed almost shocked that the man didn't believe He could heal the boy. **"Everything is possible for one who believes,"** Jesus said. This doesn't mean we will get everything we want no matter what it is as long, as we believe. It means that we must have faith in God and know He can do all things.

The question is not if God is able, the question is if we're willing to accept and trust how God is answering our prayers. God is so much bigger than us and He has things figured out better than us. Sometimes, our requests and prayers are answered in ways we don't understand or maybe even don't like, which can make it difficult to trust or believe that God really is listening to us or has our best in mind.

Next time you are praying for something, instead of praying that things go your way, pray that God is glorified, pray that God's will is done and have faith that God's plans and ways are higher than your ways. Trust that God is working things out better than we ever could and believe that while it may not be how we expect or want, God is faithful and He hears you and He is teaching you something. He will work all things out for good **(Romans 8:28).** His ways are higher and His plans are greater—have faith.

DEV. 15 | STAND IN WORSHIP

» **"For great is the LORD and most worthy of praise; he is to be feared above all gods. For all the gods of the nations are idols, but the LORD made the heavens. Splendor and majesty are before strength and glory are in his sanctuary. Ascribe to the LORD, all you families of nations, ascribe to the LORD glory and strength. Ascribe to the LORD the glory due his name; bring an offering and come into his courts." Psalm 96:4-8**

You know those moments when you're excited about something? Like really excited about it? Whether it's a new thing you've gotten, or someone you just really like, you somehow manage to fit it into every conversation, or talk about how great that person is, how funny they are, or something awesome they did.

The writer of this psalm feels that way about God and I often wonder, why don't we brag about God more? When our hearts are full of awe and wonder of God's power and might and the amazing things He's done for us, we can't help but praise His name. There are so many songs that are sung and words that are written, but sometimes we need to stop and just take in the power of God. God knows every piece of sand on the shore and put every star in the sky, yet takes the time to listen to our every thought. God, even though we've messed up more times than we can count, loved us enough to send

His Son Jesus so we never have to fear in life or in death.

We can worship God because He is living and He is working in, and through, our lives every day. While others worship gods of clay and wood **(Deuteronomy 4:28),** or of media and culture, our God was, and is, yesterday, today and forever **(Hebrews 13:8).**

Take a moment today and reflect on the might and power of God, and give Him praise. Reflect on the blessings in your life, the plan that God has for your life, the things He's taught you, the things He's brought you through—and rejoice and worship His great name. Worship that comes from a deep genuine place of thankfulness is meaningful and powerful.

DEV. 16 | STAND IN FORGIVENESS

» **"Bear with each other and forgive one another if any of you has a grievance against someone. Forgive as the Lord forgave you." Colossians 3:13**

Someone once said that unforgiveness is an open invitation for Satan to come into your heart. Not forgiving someone can be likened to drinking poison and hoping that someone else dies. Whether you believe that or not, the power of unforgiveness blurs a Biblical perspective, thwarts the purposes of God in your life, and hardens your heart.

Ever been there? Ever been disappointed? Hurt? Belittled, misunderstood, rejected by others? We have all been there and naturally we want to seek revenge, defend ourselves, and prove them wrong. However, Jesus reveals a better plan, a remedy, a kickback, a strategy to overcome the power of unforgiveness by understanding how Christ first forgave you and I.

Paul encouraged the Colossians to, **"Bear with each other and forgive one another if any of you has a grievance against someone. Forgive as the Lord forgave you."**

I encourage you to read that again. Those are powerful words.

God calls us to forgive those who have caused us grievances—those who have hurt, belittled, misunderstood, and rejected you and me. How? Why? Because God first forgave you and me while we still hated Him **(Romans 5:8).**

Honestly, whether you know or it not, you and I and everyone hated God at one time. We rejected His grace, despised His teachings, went on our own paths, and drowned out His voice. At one time, we didn't know God even though He showed His love to us.

In the same way, God calls you and me to **"bear with each other"** as Christ did for us. You see, it is easier to forgive others, even if they caused us deep pain, if we truly understand what Jesus did at the cross.

The question of today is simply this: Are you walking in a better plan or a bitter plan? Are you trying to deal with forgiveness God's way or your own way? God's way is always better. It might not be easier, but there is grace, forgiveness, freedom, and peace waiting for you as you submit to His strategy against unforgiveness.

DEV. 17 | STAND IN LOVE

» **"A new command I give you: Love one another. As I have loved you, so you must love one another. By this everyone will know that you are my disciples, if you love one another." John 13:34-35**

Everyone is looking for love. MTV plays it, countless of songwriters sing about it, and peers are saturated with finding love with someone. The filter for love is someone who is attractive or strong or popular or the whole package.

You have been there before, right? Caught in this hurricane of the world trying to find love. But very few really find it. My question to you is simply, "Is that really love?" Does MTV, the coolest and latest songwriters, your friends or classmates know what love is? Or are they really just talking about lust?

As you think about the difference between love and lust, Jesus challenges you and I this way: **"A new command I give you: Love one another. As I have loved you, so you must love one another. By this everyone will know that you are my disciples, if you love one another."**

"Love one another": one of the simplest and yet most needed commandments in our culture today. The Greek word for unconditional love is called agape love. It is a much deeper form of love than the eros (romantic) or phileo (brotherly) types of love. It is a love that goes beyond race, status, popularity, failures, and backgrounds. It is a love that changed our world.

It is easy to love people who love us. It is simple to backup family or friends in care and support, yet Jesus challenged the status quo of love and told His disciples to even love their enemies **(Matthew 5:44)**. When was the last time you revealed love to someone who hated you?

How can that possibly be a reality? Is it truly possible to love our enemies? Well, Jesus loved you and I while we hated God **(see Romans 5:8).** He took on our sins, rejection, and failures and He paved a way to encounter love. Now His followers can show radical love to others. Why? So the world would know who Jesus truly is, through you.

DEV. 18 | STAND IN JOY

» **"Consider it pure joy, my brothers and sisters, whenever you face trials of many kinds, because you know that the testing of your faith produces perseverance. Let perseverance finish its work so that you may be mature and complete, not lacking anything. If any of you lacks wisdom, you should ask God, who gives generously to all without finding fault, and it will be given to you." James 1:2-5**

Ever had a bad day?

We've all been there. Bad days occur because we live in a world that is decaying from the dominion of sin. In saying that, the Bible encourages us to consider it pure joy when we have bad days.

Bad days have a tendency to discourage us, bring out the worst in us, and sometimes ruin relationships. However, I want to encourage you that bad days weren't originally in God's plan. The book of James explains it this way:

Consider it pure joy, my brothers and sisters, whenever you face trials of many kinds, because you know that the testing of your faith produces perseverance. Let perseverance finish its work so that you may be mature and complete, not lacking anything. If any of you lacks wisdom, you should ask God, who gives generously to all without finding fault, and it will be given to you.

First, "pure joy" is deeper than the emotional happiness of eating pizza at 11 p.m. Joy is a condition: a choice that a follower of Jesus makes in every situation that comes his/her way. Why are followers of Jesus able to consider bad days as joy? Because of the reality found in salvation, the unlimited availability of His presence in our lives, and the building-up of character in Christ Jesus.

Do you consider it "pure joy" when you are having a bad day?

Second, bad days produce character—this is true discipleship! Character is built in our commitment and obedience to Christ no matter the cost **(see Luke 14:28-33).** It is a choice to trust God in the midst of a bad day so that our faith can grow, find completion in Christ, and discover wisdom beyond our natural abilities and experiences. This is possible if we rely on Christ rather than the temporary fixes in our world.

Are you relying on Christ?

DEV. 19 | STAND WITH PEACE

» **"Therefore, since we have been justified through faith, we have peace with God through our Lord Jesus Christ, through whom we have gained access by faith into this grace in which we now stand. And we boast in the hope of the glory of God." Romans 5:1-2**

"Now may the Lord of peace himself give you peace at all times and in every way. The Lord be with all of you." 2 Thessalonians 3:16

When you hear, **"STAND with Peace,"** your mind probably goes all over the place. You may assume that **STANDING** with peace means achieving and maintaining a certain level of zen in your bedroom, so you've already taken a break from reading this to go download a loop of running water and start stringing bamboo curtains. Or your mind may take you to the movement in the '60s, where tie-die was all the rage and peace and love became the necessary credo of anyone interested in being trendy. Fortunately for us, peace in the Bible is a far more substantial topic than incense and dreadlocks.

Peace is the result of Jesus dying on the cross. It has been the status of the relationship between God and humans since Jesus Christ crushed all sin. Through faith in Christ, we never have to question where we **STAND** with God again. We can have peace in our hearts.

But while God offers peace at all times and in every way, we usually decide that we would rather concern ourselves with the temporary day-to-day challenges. Though we no longer need to live with fear, stress, worry, or heartbreak, we do. We limit the effectiveness of God's peace by fixating on the present situation. Relieving pain and eliminating fear becomes our life purpose instead of revealing God's eternal peace to a world which needs it.

STANDING in the peace that God offers forces you to think outside of yourself. It allows you to see the day when all that will remain is peace. This unique and supernatural gift can fill your heart. When it does, the world around you will be changed. Creation needs you to **STAND** in the peace that has been given to you. So **STAND!**

DEV. 20 | STAND IN PATIENCE

» **"Moses answered the people, 'Do not be afraid. Stand firm and you will see the deliverance the Lord will bring you today. The Egyptians you see today you will never see again. The Lord will fight for you; you need only to be still." Exodus 14:13-15**

You are not your grandma. She hardly knows how to turn on her dusty VCR. She thinks a Celtic Celine Dion cover band CD makes a great Christmas present. She's patient. Which, if you're anything like the culture you live in, you're not! North American culture today is moving so fast that if something isn't changing or moving forward, we get nervous and think that possibly the world is about to end. There is no time for patience. Stopping means not moving and not moving means not getting anywhere. This way of thinking is a problem!

The scene in **Exodus 14** reveals one of the greatest moments in patience. Next time you feel like you need to make a decision and make it fast, consider the fact that you are not butted up against a giant river with the scariest soldiers from the most powerful empire in the world closing in on you with a plan to leave you dead for the vultures. That is the situation the Israelites found themselves in. And in the midst of it, Moses looked out to them and encouraged them with two words: **"Be still."**

"And then what, Moses? Hope they don't see us?" It seems like an incredibly difficult thing to say or hear at that moment and yet an epic miracle took place just on the other side of patience. THE SEA SPLIT OPEN. What would have happened if Moses and the Israelites kept moving instead of being patient and waiting on God's timing? Best case scenario: restored to dishonorable position of slave. Worst case: every single one of them slaughtered.

So what might you be missing out on because you are patient enough to let God lead? What miracle may be just ahead if you would only be still, not speak, and simply **STAND** in patience?

DEV. 21 | STAND IN KINDNESS

» **"And if anyone gives even a cup of cold water to one of these little ones because he is my disciple, I tell you the truth, he will certainly not lose his reward." Matthew 10:42**

"He who oppresses the poor shows contempt for their Maker, but whoever is kind to the needy honours God." Proverbs 14:31

Think of the basketball team in your school. What is the most important position? Is it the water boy? Not likely. Probably 99 percent of the students in your school could successfully fulfill the requirements of water retriever for the basketball team. In comparison, there are very few who have all the necessary prerequisites to be the star. They need a certain level of athletic ability, a lot of practice, a solid coach to teach foundational skills, and certainly a lot of support. In fact, the star needs so much support that others may have to give up some of their already limited fan base. The one carrying water to the team may, shockingly, have to fulfill his duties without any fans. Not one person chanting his name! And yet a lesson in kindness can be found in the tedious, often humbling, efforts of a water boy. Jesus teaches it in **Matthew 10:42.**

Kindness. It's the thing that everyone is capable of and no one wants to do. It's the action that rarely receives any praise or immediate reward. It's the effort that is small enough to barely be noticed and significant enough to change a life. It's goodness in action. It's getting water when someone needs water.

To **STAND** with kindness is to care for every person who needs help. You may never be promoted from water boy to superstar, but Jesus reminds us that He builds a team of water boys. **STANDING** in kindness means that you will seek out a need that anyone could take care of, you'll recognize that no one is taking care of it, and you'll **STAND** there until there is no longer a need. Does someone need a friend? Does someone need encouragement? Does someone need you to **STAND** with them? Will you **STAND?**

DEV. 22 | STAND IN GOODNESS

» **"So let's not get tired of doing what is good. At just the right time we will reap a harvest of blessing if we don't give up. Therefore, whenever we have the opportunity, we should do good to everyone—especially to those in the family of faith." Galatians 6:9-10**

I remember what it was like going to school and trying to be a person of faith. I went to youth group, I went to Historymaker, I loved Jesus, and I wanted to make a difference in my school. But when the rubber hit the road, who I was at Friday Night Youth and who I was at Monday Morning School were two different people.

Why is it so hard to be the same person at both church and school?

I remember the first person I ever tried to lead to the Lord. I got back from Historymaker charged up and ready to win the world for Jesus. I was amped. I walked into my school the next morning on the prowl, gazing down the halls like a lion looking for its prey, eyes wide open. Looking back, I probably looked more like a crazy escaped criminal searching for prison guards than a Christian teen trying to live out the Great Commission.

REFLECTION

What does living the Great Commission (Matthew 28:18-20) look like in your high school?

_____

_____

_____

_____

After what felt like hours, which in reality was only minutes into my search, there she was—my first target. Unassuming, quiet, and a little bit nerdy, she was perfect: this girl needed Jesus!

Long story short, she blew me off. She told me I was weird and too pushy and vowed never to talk to me again. I was crushed. I wanted to give up and the charge from Historymaker was gone. Truth is, the tragedy that day wasn't that this girl didn't get saved, the tragedy was that I allowed one awkward conversation to rob me of my passion. **Galatians 6:9-10** encourages us to never stop doing good. So let me encourage you, from my own mistakes: be persistent, **STAND** for Jesus, and never stop doing good.

You never know, maybe you are the catalyst that history has been waiting for. Never stop doing good. Your school needs you. Our world needs you.

What are three different ways that you can **STAND** for good in your school?

_____

_____

_____

DEV. 23 | STAND IN FAITHFULNESS

» **"Run from anything that stimulates youthful lusts. Instead, pursue righteous living, faithfulness, love, and peace. Enjoy the companionship of those who call on the Lord with pure hearts." 2 Timothy 2:22**

Dear Young Leader,

It wasn't too long ago that I was in your exact shoes. I know how difficult being a Christian in high school can be, especially when friends and faith collide in terms of peer pressure and acceptance. Nobody likes being alone, nobody likes being made fun of, and at times the tension between impressing your friends and impressing God seems unbearable.

REFLECTION
Define what it means to be cool. Why is being cool so important in high school?

_____

_____

_____

_____

The Bible does not say that being cool is from the devil, nor does it call Christian believers to be weird social outcasts. However the Bible is clear that we need to avoid the things that make us want to sin **(2 Timothy 2:22)** and if that means losing our social status, we need to be willing to say no and count the cost of our decisions.

What are some of the things God is calling you to say no to?

_____

_____

_____

_____

I strongly believe God is raising up a generation of trendsetters as opposed to trend followers—a generation of young teenage leaders, mavericks and pioneers, who are unafraid of **STANDING** up when everybody else is sitting down. I believe that you are a part of this, and I believe God is calling you to rise up, **STAND** up, and live for Jesus in your school, no matter what the cost.

The process is simple; if you want to see your life be a life of impact, listen to Jesus and do what He says. By yourself, you can accomplish little but a life surrendered in faithfulness and obedience can accomplish the impossible!

What are some of the things God is calling you to say yes to?

_____

_____

_____

_____

DEV. 24 | STAND IN GENTLENESS

» **"Since God chose you to be the holy people he loves, you must clothe yourselves with tender-hearted mercy, kindness, humility, gentleness, and patience." Colossians 3:12**

It happens to all of us. Maybe in different words or in different scenarios, but at the end of the day we'll all face one of those humiliating and embarrassing moments where somebody in the room drops a joke, everyone starts to laugh and right before you begin to join in you awkwardly realize that everyone is actually laughing at you.

REFLECTION

Has this ever happened to you or somebody you know? Looking back, how did you feel about how everything went down?

_____

_____

_____

_____

The Christian question to ask would be, "WWJD?" How do we stand for our faith when people make fun of us? I would love to tell you that Jesus would have responded with an epic roundhouse kick to the head single-handedly (or footedly) knocking out the wise guy, but unfortunately that isn't found in the Gospels.

What are the most practical ways you can help take a **STAND** against bullying in your school?

_____

_____

_____

_____

Like it or not, our world is full of lame-o, wannabe comedians, and insensitive meatheads who pick on everyone around them. What attitude should we adopt to make a reverse impact on the bully and an eternal impact in our school? The answer can be found in **Colossians 3:12.** Believe it or not there is an incredible amount of life-changing and life-giving authority in words like kindness, gentleness, humility and patience. I know it seems nuts, but give it a try: you will be surprised by the results!

What does responding with an attitude of gentleness actually look like when faced with a situation like this? In what ways would responding with these types of attitudes affect the situation?

_____

_____

_____

_____

DEV. 25 | STAND IN SELF-CONTROL

» **"Therefore, prepare your minds for action; be self-controlled; set your hope fully on the grace to be given you when Christ is revealed." I Peter 1:13**

When I was younger, I would sometimes wait until the rest of my family was sleeping, sneak into the kitchen, and find the coveted cookie jar full of cookies. I'd grab one cookie and quietly tip toe back to my room where I would devour it as if I was trying to set a new world record.

As we find ourselves getting older, we are continually confronted with decisions where we desperately need to live in self-control. As a child, we did not fully understand self-control and the need for it, but as we move from those childish issues to grown-up ones, self-control helps us guard against bad influences and decisions.

Self-control is an action word that causes us to make a choice: "Do I allow myself to watch something that I know I shouldn't?", "Should I go to my friend's house knowing we will being experimenting with drugs?", "Am I going to cheat on my exam because I didn't study?" We need to allow Christ to strengthen our self-control in both the small things and in the larger ones. As we allow Christ and self-control to guide us, we will feel encouraged and move forward.

REFLECTION
Think back to the last time you needed to make

a decision that took self-control. How did you feel afterwards? What are the areas in your life right now that you need to have self-control in? Today, prepare for action as you allow Christ to give you the self-control you need to bring honour and glory to Him in all that you do.

DEV. 26 | STAND PRAYERFULLY

» "Devote yourselves to prayer, being watchful and thankful." Colossians 4:2

"Do not be anxious about anything, but in everything, by prayer and petition, with thanksgiving, present your requests to God." Philippians 4:6

"And pray in the Spirit on all occasions with all kinds of prayers and requests. With this in mind, be alert and always praying for all the saints." Ephesians 6:18

You want to have a crazy life? Learn how to pray.

Throughout history, humanity has seen how God works through prayer. Prayer has the ability to heal the sick, feed the hungry, cast out worry, and comfort, energize and change your very own life. For many people, prayer is something that is done only around the dinner table when we need to bless the Christmas turkey. But for a disciple, it is a lifestyle that we have been called to pursue and be active in.

When we look at prayer in the Bible it is evident that not only are we are called to pray, but we are also to do things like **"pray without ceasing"** and **"continue to pray."** Prayer is an ongoing part of who we are as Christians. As disciples of Christ, we have the calling and ability to come to

God in prayer not only in quietness and in solitude, but also when we are traveling to school or work and living throughout the day. Many times I have prayed while sitting in my car waiting for a stoplight to change color, or even while standing in a grocery line. The point is that no matter where we are, we need to continue to have a mindset that is submersed in prayer.

REFLECTION

What are the areas in your life or a friend's life where you long to see God work? This week, spend some time intentionally praying for those around you (even being specific), being watchful and thankful to God as He hears and answers prayers.

» "Be on your guard; stand firm in the faith; be men of courage; be strong. Do everything in love." I Corinthians 16:13

What makes a man anyways? Muscles and hormones? Burping and farting? A life of conquest ... in video games? Hard to say, unless we know more about our true identity and design.

The world we live in has all kinds of ideas and messages it sends about what it means to be male. But, just like no one knows the exact ingredients in a great meal like the chef who made it, no one knows the exact design details of creation like the Creator. The Creator knows best!

Guys–your identity isn't just rooted in being human, but in being male! **Genesis 1:27 says, "God created human beings in His own image ... male and female he created them" (NLT).** God is a farmer and He has planted all kinds of great seeds in the soil of our lives. He is making an impressive landscape from your life that displays the qualities of a man of God. In you He's planted a variety of things that reflect awesome elements of His heart and nature. Things like strength and compassion, confidence and humility, courage and truth, selflessness and zeal.

Some of these seeds burst through the surface of your life long ago and are very productive, others are still taking root and you'll see them grow even more in the future.

The Bible has so many great things that affirm you as a guy. Perhaps one of the best passages says, **"Be on your guard; stand firm in the faith; be men of courage; be strong. Do everything in love" (I Corinthians 16:13).** How does God want to encourage you today? This Scripture tells us about four ways.

First, He's reminding you to be on your guard. All kinds of outside pressures would like to subtly cause you to think less of God, less of women, and less of yourself. Stop thoughts like those right in their tracks! Second, God is inviting you to **STAND** in the most important place you can—a place of firm faith! Nothing is more important in life than a meaningful friendship with God. What could you do today that would bring even more strength to your faith in Jesus? Third, God wants you to know that you can be known as a man of courage and strength. The kind of muscles God is talking about here are rooted in Him and are seen when you flex things like integrity and solid character. Step up and **STAND** out today! Lastly, God is assuring you that true manliness expresses itself in love. Love is putting others first. Love is bold in its generosity. Start by practicing love where it matters most, at home and with family. Doing that can be a challenge, but without a doubt you're man enough!

Our world is waiting for guys to really live like the men God has made them to be. **STAND** as a man!

» Your teen and young adult years can be best times of your life as you learn all about this new adventure called womanhood. You're becoming your own person and who God has made you to be. I heard some wise words when I was in my teens: "Who you commit to being now will be who you end up being later." I have found this wisdom to be true.

Every day, you are being formed and discipled by one of two sources: today's culture or God Himself. Many try to take a bit of both—whichever suits their desire for the moment, but both want your full attention. You can only play them both for so long before one gets jealous. The question is: who do you want to be in the end? Let's take a look at two women who took two different paths and see if we can learn something from them.

Proverbs 7 describes a woman who is drop dead gorgeous. She's got her designer jeans on and lookin' fine. She's dressed to impress, and it's working. She's out on the town and ready to find herself a hot guy. She spots him. There's no waiting with her, she's got her eyes ready for the full-on flirt. She's studied all the looks that work on luring the guy she wants. Her friends are amazed at her strategy. She flips her hair just right as he approaches her. She's got him right where she wants him. Without waiting another moment, she grabs him and kisses him. Whoa, she works fast! She invites him home with her and he follows in hot pursuit.

Long before the Pussycat Dolls sang about "loosening up their buttons," there were women who were rebellious, stubborn, dressing sexy to attract attention, and getting their ego stroked by how many men they could attract. But there's more to this woman's story. She happens to be a Christian. She even assures her new man that she went to "church" before she came to get him. There's more still; she's married. Her husband is out of town. Move over Desperate Housewives! The problem is that she's deceived by her own foolishness. While she's enjoying her rebellion and independence, her very soul is being lost.

Why does this matter to you? If you're rebellious and promiscuous in heart before you're married, unless you change of where you're getting your discipleship from, it won't be any different with a ring on. Proverbs talks a lot about wisdom, where it comes from, and the importance of what goes into your heart. **Proverbs 4:23 says, "Keep vigilant watch over your heart; for that's where life starts" (The Message).** How do you do that? You're careful what you see and hear, because those things go straight into your heart and becomes what disciples you. Listen to music that encourages promiscuity long enough and you'll see it impact your life. Every day, music, TV, and other media seek to win your attention. It wants to blur your spiritual eyesight so you can no longer see right from wrong. It numbs you from being able to hear God's voice. The book of Proverbs encourages an alternative; to allow God's Word to be written on your very soul. What a difference it makes.

Proverbs 31 shows us what a woman looks like when she's been discipled by Christ; when she's taken good care of her heart. She's a keeper. No really, she's a keeper because a woman this good is hard for a man to find. Her value is greater than diamonds. Her man trusts her to be faithful to him when he's away. He trusts her to not look after her own selfish desires, but for the good of the whole family. She's energetic and inventive. She helps provide for the family by making wise choices with her money. She's confident in her beauty. She doesn't fall for the latest beauty trends that cost a ton of money. She invests her money in things that make profit, like buying land. There's not a lazy bone in her body. She gets up in the morning ready to seize the day using the talents she's been given. She makes the world a better place. She rebels against the popular culture by avoiding "me, me, me" mindsets, and serving the poor and outcast instead. The words that come out of her mouth are kind and build the people around her rather than trading the latest gossip. Her husband and kids adore her. Why wouldn't they! She has taken good care of her heart and is impacting her family and the world around her as a result.

But perhaps the biggest compliment shared about her is that she fears God. No, she's not scared of God, but she has given Him first place in her heart and she obeys Him—even when it's hard. She believes something that other women miss: that beauty only goes so far, but it's a woman who has given God her full surrender who is worthy of praise.

Girls, you get one shot at this life before you stand before your Creator. Don't waste any time with the worthless things this culture offers. It looks good on the outside, but it will only leave your soul empty and your heart calloused and hard. Take good care of your heart by feeding it things that will draw out your love for your Heavenly Father. Inside of you is God's answer to a dying world. To be consumed by the world only hinders you from ever seeing what God could do with your life.

STAND strong in your heart.
STAND against messages that are contrary to what's written in God's Word.
STAND firm on what God says.
STAND in the beauty He has created you in.
STAND up for the poor, broken and outcast.
STAND against messages that only seek to feed the god of self.
STAND against getting your esteem from attention from guys and back onto the Father.
STAND when you feel you can't **STAND** any longer.

Because who God is building you into now is who you will grow to be in the future. Live with tomorrow in mind.

STAND
IN LEADERSHIP

» Many people have various definitions when it comes to leadership but it is simply a fact that "Leadership is influence."

Now, not all influence is healthy or good. Some influence is evil: the concentration camps in World War II and the genocide in Rwanda are just a couple of examples. In addition, there is selfish leadership. In the 2008 stock market crash, leaders of Fortune 500 companies such as GM, AIG, and others were motivated by greed and selfish gain rather than making their businesses, the economy, and ultimately the world a better place.

Healthy leadership is exemplified through Christ. If He was online today, He would have the most Twitter followers in the world. Jesus' influence resonates through His words, actions, and methods. His impact has outperformed any other leader in history, including Martin Luther King Jr., Obama, or Wayne Gretzky. He is worthy to follow.

In saying that, Jesus teaches us a plethora of leadership principles. But the most important leadership lesson is this: A great leader who is positive, effective for life change, and makes an everlasting difference on this earth needs to be a great follower.

Let me say that again: a great leader is first a great follower.

You may ask yourself why this would be the case. Isn't a leader someone who is followed? That is true, but while leadership is usually influenced by human emotions, ambitions, inspirations, or desires, Jesus shows us a better way to lead.

First, the Gospels reveal Jesus did nothing without the Father's permission. He performed miracles, chose the twelve disciples, spoke in the temples, and reclined with sinners in correlation with the Father's will: **"I'm telling you this straight. The Son can't independently do a thing, only what he sees the Father doing.**

What the Father does, the Son does. The Father loves the Son and includes him in everything he is doing" (John 5:19, the Message).

This phenomenon indicates the special, active, and dynamic relationship Jesus had with the Father. This is a good time to pause and think: "What motivates me as a leader?" Is it greed that says, "What's in it for me?" Is it based on selfishness? Or is it based on the Father's will for your life, "How can I glorify God?"

Please read over that again, because it is a foundational question to leadership. You see, if we aren't motivated by the Father's will for our lives in leadership, then we are motivated by the opinions of people and/ or by our own selfish emotions and desires.

If popularity motivates us, we will compromise our own integrity, confidence, and convictions to gain it. An example of this is King Solomon **(1 Samuel 9-15).** Solomon was considered the wealthiest, wisest, and most popular dude alive in his day. He had nations follow him, kings and queens adore him, and gained respect by so many that he had little accountability in his leadership responsibilities. For example, he started to take his leadership matters in his own hands by intermarrying with women from different religions to create treaties with pagan nations. In his own eyes, this was a wise move, but in God's eyes, it was going to cost him his relationship with God. Ultimately, King Solomon was being moved by his intermarriages against his relationship with God and became desensitized to His ways. He counterfeited his relationship with God to build his own popularity.

Furthermore, if selfish emotions and desires get in the way, we miss what God wants to do in and through us. The Pharisees, the crowds, and ultimately some of Jesus' disciples believed Jesus was going to set up an earthly Kingdom. Their hope was for Jesus to bring down Rome and therefore establish Himself as a ruling, conquering Messiah. As you and I know, Jesus' Kingdom is bigger than any earthly kingdom as He established a spiritual one in our hearts (that will eventually become earthly in eternity). People had selfish motives for Jesus. Furthermore, Jesus could have given in to those selfish desires but He didn't, because He never wavered from His special, active, and dynamic relationship with the Father.

In the same way, if you and I want to become great leaders who make an eternal, positive, and life-changing difference on this earth, we need to have a special, active, and dynamic relationship with Jesus.

Second, Jesus reveals to you and I what a dynamic relationship with God looks like. In the Gospels, Jesus set out a template of what it means to have a relationship with God. He had regular times of prayer, listening and meditating with God. Mark indicates that Jesus went in the morning while it was still dark to go and pray in solitude **(Mark 1:35).** Luke reveals that Jesus often withdrew to a private place to pray **(Luke 5:16).**

Jesus–who was sinless, Almighty God, the Saviour of the World, God's Son–cleared His calendar to pray, refocus His priorities, and align Himself with the Father to pray. How much more do you and I need to pray?

In addition, Jesus knew the Scriptures. He was a student of the active and living Word of God. Before you breeze through this important aspect of Jesus, you need to reflect on how Jesus used the Scriptures. He quoted them to thwart Satan during the tests in the desert **(Matthew 4),** enriched the Law through the Sermon on the Mount **(Matthew 5-7),** preached it in the synagogues **(Matthew 4:23; 9:35; 13:54),** and ultimately fulfilled it through His works **(Matthew 8)** and the cross **(Matthew 26:1-27:66).**

Jesus knew the power of the Scriptures. He knew the active Word which penetrates every motive, convicts the deepest darkest parts of the human heart, transforms people into the likeness of God, and thwarts the purposes of evil in this world. Without the active Word of God living in them, a leader is like someone who tries to walk a path in the dead dark of night without a flashlight.

Ultimately, we need to ask ourselves: are we applying the Word of God to our personal lives? Is it active, breathing, convicting, revealing, and refreshing our souls?

Furthermore, Jesus revealed His dependence on the Holy Spirit in His daily life. The baptism of Jesus before His public ministry, as recorded in **Matthew 3:13-17, Mark 1:9-11, Luke 3:21-22, and John 1:29-34,** explains the empowerment of God one needs before going into leadership. The sign is found in a dove descending on Jesus and the Father proclaiming, **"This is my Son; whom I am well pleased."** Jesus reveals by His example the need for the Holy Spirit in our lives.

He promised His disciples that they would never be alone but would be infused with the Holy Spirit as a sign for ministry in witness, empowerment, boldness, overcoming sin, and living in unity with one another **(Acts 1:8; Galatians 5:16-18).**

Leadership can be lonely because leading your peers at youth group, schools, sports teams, and other places is all about your example. Talk is cheap, and sometimes people, parents, and even the devil try to test our talk to see if the actions will follow. Honestly, this is where the true test of leadership lies: will yours actions follow your words?

Be encouraged! The Holy Spirit that created the heavens and earth, performed miracles, signs and wonders throughout the ages, and resurrected Jesus from the dead, now dwells in you! In other words, Jesus is with you. You are never alone in an active, living, and dynamic relationship with God. This is good news.

Third, and simply put, Jesus reveals the need for unity **(John 17:21)**. In other words, spiritual leaders are called to bring out the best in others and to make the world a better place, by pointing people to Jesus and His agenda for the world **(Matthew 28:16-20).** I love the fact that Jesus never took any of the glory; He always deflected praise to the Father. Leadership, in the same way, is to bring glory to God because every other motive, emotion, inspiration, goal, vision statement, or gift/talent/ability is futile compared to what God has in store for those who love Him **(I Corinthians 2:9).**

In addition, unity speaks of teamwork. It deflects glory from me and you to each other. It is about bringing out the best in each other to make our world a better place. This truly is the heart of Christ.

REFLECTION
How are you bringing out the best in others?

_____

_____

_____

True leadership is following God through Jesus Christ. He revealed to the world the foundational truth that a leader needs to be first a great follower.

» "Greater love has no one than this: to lay down one's life for one's friends." John 15:12

Most friendships are filled with conditions. You might have heard something like this before: "I will invite her if she invites me," "We're not friends anymore because she made fun of me," or "He never helps me, why should I help him?". As long as people are nice to us, we will be nice to them. As long as our friends are good to us, we will be good to them. This is normal.

Jesus shows a different way—a better way. Consider Jesus' friendship with you. Even when you do not love Him, He loves you. When you turn your back on Him, lie to Him, break promises, and speak poorly of Him, He stays the same: faithful, kind, loving and willing to start over. Imagine if we treated our friends like this.

Jesus challenges us to love each other in the same way that He loves us. We **STAND** when we become friends with people like Jesus is friends with us. No matter how we are treated, we are the same: kind, loving, and available. Imagine how much these friendships would **STAND** out. When we become this kind of friend, we point people to the best friendship they could ever have: a friendship with Jesus Christ.

When I was 19 the girl I was dating dumped me. I was in love and saving up for a ring when she broke up with me. My heart hurt so bad I thought I was going to explode. The weird thing is, my friend Jared took it almost as bad as I did. I was depressed and so was he. He made me a break-up mix and we would listen to it on our drive to university. We would go get spicy chickens from Wendy's and just sit. This is what Paul was talking about in Romans when he said, **"rejoice with those who are rejoicing and mourn with those that are mourning."**

Good friends **STAND** with friends when things are good and when things are bad. When our friends get a good grade, we celebrate. We don't need to be jealous because they are doing better in school or have a higher paying job, we celebrate because a win for a friend is a win for us. In the same way, a loss for a friend is a loss for us. The good thing about that kind of friendship is this: no one needs to celebrate alone and no one needs to cry alone.

» God created family. It was very early on that He decided that **"it was not good for man to be alone."** So woman was created and man and woman were told to go and populate the earth. They were meant to go and become family.

As time carried on, family structure changed and morphed repeatedly. Yet enduring all of this change is the fact that family is still close to the heart of God. Specific instructions are given to parents, children, nieces, nephews, brothers and sisters throughout Scripture about family. And possibly none were clearer than God's instruction to Moses and the Israelites in the Ten Commandments.

In **Exodus 20,** God gives the Israelites ten rules, or commandments, to live by. These rules become the backbone of the Law of Moses, which Israel followed religiously for thousands of years. Within that law is written the instruction to, **"Honour your Father and your Mother."**

This law was given to a nation of religious people with extreme family values. It was through this family structure that faith was passed on. A large portion of honouring your father and mother would have included receiving, with an open heart, the faith of the family. It was through the family that God reminded the Israelites of His miracles, through the family that God established His people, and through the family that God is remembered.

Honouring your father and mother meant that you would remain in obedience to God. Yet you may look at your parents and realize that if you lived a life that stands for their values and beliefs, you would be disobeying God. Many parents in North American culture are not prioritizing obedience to God in their life goals. Fifty percent of people reading this have divorced parents—that's not what God wants for your life!

A student who decides they are going to **STAND** for Jesus will have far greater dreams for this culture than to simply live out the faith of their parents. **STANDING** means refusing to conform to the patterns of this world, and in doing so, realizing that the values and faith of the past generation is not enough. The faith that will make a difference in the culture today has to be passionate, bold, and creative, something that, on a whole, will not be learned from the previous generation.

The faith that this generation needs to **STAND** on must be passed down from God, not people! This will lead to a generation who reprioritizes the way they spend their time, money and efforts. Some parents won't agree with this reprioritization, which gives you a very unique opportunity. You may choose to rebel, write off your parents as faithless, criticize who they are and how they've raised you, and call it an act of obedience to God—or you could become the person that the world needs. One who maybe has difficult times in family, who maybe believes different things than their family, but who is willing to **STAND** for, not against, their family.

The person that will impact their family now and in the future is not the person who acquires such a faith that it causes them to rebel against anything or anyone that they don't want to become. The person that will impact their family is the one who **STANDS** for God in their family and not against their family for God. The greatest motivation you should have is not to **STAND** against anything, but to **STAND** for God. Don't be inspired by who you will avoid becoming, but by who you can become.

You may have divorced parents, atheist parents, compromising parents, messed up parents, overachieving parents, careless parents, strict parents, overly religious parents, or you may have good parents—but I can guarantee you don't have perfect parents. Rather than criticizing them, God is asking you to **STAND**. Receive God's love fully so that you will love your family sincerely. As love grows in your heart, it prepares you to lead and love your future spouse and your family well. **STAND!**

You may have a parent who struggles with homosexuality or they may have another belief or religion. In light of knowing Jesus yourself, you may wonder how they could ever be the way they are. Jesus loves them and so can you. Show them love. Strive to become like Jesus and let your light shine. You can't change a heart, but He can. **STAND!**

If you have been mistreated by your family in the past and think that you deserve revenge or should be allowed to hold bitterness in your heart, God wants to restore you, and it will never be through hurting another. **STAND.** If one of your siblings has been favoured over you and you feel like you are not treated fairly, God has given you more than you need and wants to give you even more. Your parents can't give you as much as He can. **STAND!** If you feel like you have a greater faith than your parents, **STAND** in humility. Comparison is not a gift from God. You are not **STANDING** against anything; you're **STANDING** for God. **STAND!** If you have never felt like God could use you, **STAND.** Whatever has been told to you, or whatever role model you've had, God calls you to **STAND!**

REFLECTION

There are many Bible verses that deal with family (Exodus 20:12, Ephesians 6:1-2, Proverbs 31, Psalm 103:17, Genesis 2:24, Proverbs 22:6, Ephesians 5:21-33, Proverbs 22:6). Take some time to read them. Ask God to give you wisdom and understanding for your family. Also take some time to pray for your future spouse and your future family. Think about the kind of Godly principles that you will one day build your own marriage and family on. Write these things down and begin to pray regularly about them.

STAND
AS A REBEL

» Righteous and rebel. Do those words even go together? Visions of "righteous" bring images of nuns to my mind. "Rebel" makes me think of skipping school. Put those two things together and you've got a nun skipping school … hmmm, that's not really what we're talking about.

We're all looking for adventure, a thrill that makes life a little more interesting than math class. I get it. When life seems dull, I'm off to find an edge to live on. Unfortunately in my past, I spent far too long living on the wrong edge. The edge of ambition, wanting popularity and success, only left me in the dust. The edge of pursuing beauty and dancing my nights away in the club only emptied my soul. I was on the wrong edge. I was a rebel without a cause.

Do you feel the same? Do you wonder what your alternative is? Running to a church and watching the same scene happen week after week: sing, sit, listen, text friends during the sermon you don't get. Longing to do the right thing and make a difference for God, you feel you should attend church, but find something is missing. You find yourself on another edge of boredom, comfort, confined in a bubble that is somewhat disappointing.

Whoa, wait a minute! Let's not bash the church! If what they say is true, that church is you and I—not just a building—then maybe it's not the church that is supposed to serve the experiences we so desire on a silver platter. Maybe the key to being a "righteous rebel" is to first get rebellious about the right things, and allow that to infect everyone else around us. Instead of seeing church and Christianity as something like robotic action, maybe we're meant to be instigators of a holy riot?

So what are the right things to rebel against? What does a holy riot look like? First off, there's a key that gives us the eyes to see what needs a little rebellion. It's "the fear of the Lord" that's talked about in Proverbs. What did that statement just do inside of you? Lots of times we think it means being scared of God, but it's not. Very simply, to "fear God" means to love what He loves and hate what He hates.

God "hates"? Really? Yup. There are some things He hates, and He wants those who follow Him to hate the same things. So what are they? **Proverbs 6:16-20 (The Message)** tells us:

Here are six things God hates, and one more that he loathes with a passion: eyes that are arrogant, a tongue that lies, hands that murder the innocent, a heart that hatches evil plots, feet that race down a wicked track, a mouth that lies under oath, a troublemaker in the family.

Did you get that? He intensely despises those things. He finds them morally disgusting. Maybe we should too.

Maybe we need to start rebelling against eyes that want to look down on others because they're different or uncool. Maybe we need to rebel against the judgment in our hearts towards those we don't understand. Maybe we need to stop worshipping the wrong god of self.

Maybe we need to rebel against ourselves and our own selfishness that shows up in lies. Lies are deceit. It speaks of fooling ourselves to believe things we want to be true but really aren't! We need to riot against our own heart that says it loves God but then lives a completely different way. It's time to say "No more!" to lifeless words that have no reality in our lives. God is sick of it.

Maybe it's time for us to rebel against the defenses of our hearts that want to put the blame on others for the suffering in our world? Hasn't God called us to be a representation of His answer? Enough of the bubble we live in, all cozy with our iPhones, designer jeans, and bling. What about our world in crisis? If you knew 30,000 children died in your own country in the last three months, would you blink? It's happening right now in the horn of Africa. Do we care? Or does the love of our own selves blind us? Inside of you lies an answer and a passion for God's cause: a righteous rebel who says NO MORE.

Maybe if we got rebellious towards the things that move God's heart to disgust, we wouldn't have time for our own rebellion? We wouldn't have time to imagine the dreams and desires for our own lives, but would be consumed with God's dream for His earth.

What would happen to the church Jesus dreamed of starting if we fostered this kind of rebellion? The world as we know it would be transformed. Don't wait any longer. We need your rebellion. Stop looking to others to do it and start it yourself. When young people step up to the plate, adults take notice. You are more inspiring than you know!

STAND-OFF to the status quo, bust out of mediocrity, and do a full-on sprint to the edge of a new ideal: His ideal. His dream for His Kingdom to come on earth. Be rebellious towards the right things: injustice, hatred, jealousy, greed, status, and consumerism. It's time that God, rather than culture, defines our reality.

Ready for the rebellion?

REFLECTION

Brainstorm a list of things you will no longer **STAND** for in your life, in your school, and in our world. Then pray and ask God to show you how you can practically **STAND** in a positive way to be a righteous rebel. Remember no step is too small to begin taking a **STAND**.

PROBLEM	ACTION
Gossip	Be an encourager
Homelessness	Serve at a downtown mission

STAND
IN SEXUAL TEMPTATION

» "When you are tempted, God will provide a way out so you can stand up under it." I Corinthians 10:13

Sex is a creation of God, and there is nothing dirty about it. God designed sexuality to be an exciting and blessed part of life for people. Can you imagine if God created something as powerful as sex but didn't warn of the dangers of misuse or tell us about the context it is intended for? That would be unfair! God wants the best for us and the Bible shows us that sex is for two people of the opposite gender within the safety of a committed marriage relationship. Like always, the enemy tries to pervert what God created to be good, suggesting alternatives and imitations that fall way short of the real thing and always lead to pain, regret and broken relationships. So how should we respond when we feel tempted sexually?

It is important to remember that temptation isn't sin; it is a reality in life. Even Jesus experienced all kinds of temptation **(Hebrews 2:18 and 4:15).** If you ever feel tempted, don't get down on yourself, look to God instead. In **I Corinthians 10:13,** we read, **"God is faithful; He will not let you be tempted beyond what you can bear. But when you are tempted, He will provide a way out so you can stand up under it."** This means when you approach temptation with God you can be sure the temptation, no matter how strong it may seem, doesn't have to overpower you! This Scripture also tells us that there is always a way out of a tempting situation. If you get tempted, give your head a shake and look for the way out! Click the 'x', turn off the TV, stop texting that person, listen to some worship songs, say something to the other person, or end a relationship if you have to—whatever it takes! Don't bother trying to fight temptation face to face, instead run from it! **(I Corinthians 6:18-20)**

One of the worst temptations anyone could ever experience isn't even sexual. It is the temptation we experience when we have messed up in some way. We might be tempted to hide from God or hide our sin somehow. Remember how Adam and Eve tried both? Instead, like the prodigal son, we need to remember that God the Father is good and that when we run to Him to **"confess our sins to Him, He is faithful and just to forgive us our sins and cleanse us" (1 John 1:9, NLT).** Someone once said that purity isn't a destination, it's a direction. That means if someone fails in some way, the best thing to do is to get up, go to God, let Him forgive, cleanse, and show you His life-changing love. Then keep close to Him and keep walking on the purity path, trusting that His way is best and the dreams He has for every area of your life are better than you could imagine **(Ephesians 3:20).**

STAND
IN TIMES OF TESTING

» **"Consider it a sheer gift, friends, when tests and challenges come at you from all sides. You know that under pressure, your faith-life is forced into the open and shows its true colors. So don't try to get out of anything prematurely. Let it do its work so you become mature and well-developed, not deficient in any way." (James 1:2-4 The Message)**

You **STAND** there. Don't let anything move you. When winds of doubt threaten to throw you off your place, you plant your feet firmer. When obstacles hurl themselves towards you, duck—but don't back down. **STAND** there. When you are about to be pushed over by the weight of hardship, lean in and push back against it.

It's harder to **STAND** than to move. Try **STANDING** in one spot and not moving for fifteen minutes, thirty minutes, an hour … it's hard. Likewise, it's hard to **STAND** and resist the temptation to **STAND** in your own power, to face your doubt square in the face. To be honest with your inner emotion, to have the courage to hand it over into the hands of a loving God, to believe. To still believe beyond the shadow of a doubt that He is what says He is. It goes against the very fabric of our culture to **STAND** and still believe when the message everywhere is to run to things that will help make it all better: shopping, another relationship, being popular, an iPhone, the image a group of friends can bring, a new shade of lipstick … but all it does is keep us in its grip, only to repeat the cycle again. It leaves us empty.

Can you still believe that He is love, that He is good, and that He is kind, despite what's happened to you? Can you have enough faith to believe in God's complete ability to restore your life? Even further, can you have enough faith to believe that in the meantime brokenness can bring life to you greater than you've known—fellowship with Jesus and His sufferings?

Suffering is a word that our culture avoids at all costs because it goes right against the god of self.

Do you blame yourself? Do you think it's because you somehow haven't met God's ideals? Do you feel you fell short and He's punishing you? I went through a season like that. I lost a job I loved, my father passed away suddenly from cancer, and three months later, I unexpectedly lost my grandma who I was very close to. All I was left with was doubt.

The next few years I lost more: my grandpa, the hip hop business I started from the ground up, almost all of my friends, and the hardest hit of all: moving to a new city, bringing me to the loneliest place I've ever been. I thought God had left me. I was numb. I wanted to live for Him, but felt I was no longer invited. All I could say to God for two years was, "I'm so sorry." I could only pray He would hear me. Too bad I didn't stick around long enough to hear His response.

What do you do when your life isn't turning out the way you thought? Where's God? Maybe there's more to suffering and this life than we think? Looking back, I can see the depth brokenness and hardship created in my life. That depth wasn't there before. Mountaintops give great views, but it's the climb that builds the muscles. It's no different in our spiritual walk. You can't always have the spiritual high. At some point, tension needs to make you stronger. So, back to the question: will you stand and stay **STANDING**?

It takes guts to **STAND** through the challenges. And just because the verse says the end result is being mature and well-developed doesn't mean you can't be honest about the journey. Once I finally realized God didn't hate me, I was truthful with Him about my emotions—my grief, my disappointment, my pain, and my anger. He was able to handle it. It actually helped me get through.

I want to know Christ—yes, to know the power of His resurrection and participation in His sufferings, becoming like Him in his death **(Philippians 3:10).**

When we "participate in His sufferings," we get to know Him more. Is that the cry of your heart; to know Him? Are you willing to allow suffering to bring you closer to Him, rather than cause your heart to run from Him? Are you willing to see suffering as an asset rather than something to detest? That's probably one of our biggest challenges as rebels to the culture—to have the guts to participate with Christ in suffering, and to do it willingly. Who does that?

It will take more courage than you know you have, but you do have it. Don't quit. More than ever, get yourself into His Word and find a community of other Jesus-followers to pray and support you. Dare to **STAND** firm and let nothing move you. Dare to be the Christ-follower that isn't afraid to partake in His sufferings.

And when you have done everything to **STAND**, **STAND** some more.

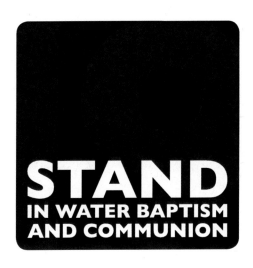

STAND
IN WATER BAPTISM
AND COMMUNION

» "A final word: Be strong in the Lord and in His mighty power." Ephesians 6:10

On every car, every shoe, and on every t-shirt, there are symbols and logos and brands that we all instantly recognize. Some of these symbols show the world how cool, hip, and trendy we are while some of the logos that we choose to wear make other people think we're lame. Some of these symbols identify you to a certain cause or show your support for a certain hockey team, but no matter what, symbols mean something.

Some symbols infuriate us, right? Have you ever been in traffic driving your busted-up old beater car when you spotted someone waving one finger at you? That's a symbol that causes us anger. Other symbols, however, make us really happy. The golden arches, for example, symbolize cheap, tasty food and, if you need it, a job.

Symbols also have a tendency to identify us. Other people can learn a little bit about who we are based on the symbols and logos and brands that we identify with. Symbols are actually a type of language. In fact, the words you are reading right now are just symbols typed on paper that point to big ideas and pictures. Symbols are a language that helps us to understand other things.

And that's the great thing about symbols: they always point us to something else.

When my wife and I were married, we exchanged wedding rings as a symbol of devotion and love to one another. It shouldn't come as a surprise then that when I take my ring off we don't cease to be married and I don't stop loving her. When I put the ring back on we don't need to get re-married, re-honeymooned, and re-newlywedded. The ring is simply a symbol and symbols always point to something greater than itself.

That is what water baptism and communion are—symbols. They are symbols that point us to something much greater.

WATER BAPTISM

Water baptism is an interesting symbol that identifies us with Jesus and is an important step in the discipleship process. While water baptism does not make you a Christian, both Jesus **(Matthew 28:19)** and his Apostles **(Acts 2:38)** command that Christians should be baptized. What this means is that when you commit your life to following Jesus, a natural and normal part of that process is water baptism.

Water baptism doesn't mean that you have your life all figured out or that you're perfect. It doesn't mean that you understand everything in the Bible or even agree with everything that a preacher says. Rather, baptism is a public declaration–a symbol–that you have put the life of Jesus ahead of your own and that you are aligning your life to look more like His.

The word for baptism, in its original Biblical language, described something that had been submerged under water. It was a word often used to describe ships and boats that had sunk or had become immersed underwater. In part, this is where we get our modern practice of dunking people under water when we baptize them.

In the ancient world, however, Christianity wasn't the only religion that dunked people under water in baptism.

Some pagan religions from around the same time as Jesus and the early church practiced a form of baptism. If you were to convert to this pagan religion, you would be held under water flailing and thrashing for air before going limp and passing out. Just before you died, you'd be brought up and out of the water to simulate a death and new life experience. Quite literally, you would be given a new life.

The Jewish culture adopted the practice of baptism as well, though they didn't hold people underwater until they passed out. Converts to the Jewish faith would be baptized to symbolize a new and cleansed life. In fact, Orthodox Jews still practice this today.

From there, Jesus and the early church adopted the Jewish custom of baptism to be a symbol of new life. When people became believers in Jesus, they would be baptized in this way. This baptism was a symbol that identified Christians with Jesus.

Baptism, in all of its various forms, points to something much larger than willingly being dunked in water or splashed in the face. They say that a picture is worth a thousand words and baptism is the picture of Jesus' death and resurrection. It doesn't make you a Christian to be baptized but it is a symbol of what has already happened in your life identifying you as belonging to Jesus and His church. You are identifying with Jesus in His death (dying to yourself), His burial (dying to your old way of life), and His resurrection (living by the power of His Holy Spirit).

In baptism, what you are saying is that you are being immersed into the life of Christ. **"Having been buried with him in baptism, in which you were also raised with him through your faith in the working of God, who raised him from the dead."(Colossians 2:12)**

There are many things that we can immerse our lives into: writing music, social networks, working hard, or fulfilling some sexual fantasy. We can be immersed in our selfishness, our pride, our books and learning, our experiences, substance abuse, relationships, or just plain survival. We can be immersed into any culture, any lifestyle, and any sin. Jesus wants each of us to be immersed in Him; immersed into who He is and what He is about.

That's the symbol of baptism. Our old way of living needs

to die and this new way of living, this new life in Christ, is what we are being immersed into. As Christians, part of what we are doing in baptism is making a public commitment to follow Jesus well. There is nothing magical or mystical about baptism, but a couple of things do happen.

First, expect to be changed. Because baptism is part of discipleship, there are going to be changes happening in your life. God the Holy Spirit will be speaking to you and convicting you on certain parts of your life that don't line up with Scripture. What it means to be a follower of Jesus is that your life begins to look more and more like His. In baptism, part of what you are saying is "I'm willing to be changed."

Second, expect to be challenged. Baptism is a symbol of your followership with Jesus. As Christians we do that in community, with other people. We are in Christian community so that other people can speak into our lives, challenge us on our issues, and help us see our blind spots. The Christian community, the church, has more responsibility and more right to speak into your life to confront and challenge sin in your life, in a caring way. Discipleship means walking side-by-side with other Christians and inviting them into our lives to help us follow Jesus better.

So the big question: How do you know that you should be baptized? If you answer "yes" to both of the following questions, please talk to your youth pastor or youth leader, a parent, or another mature Christian:

1. Are you a Christian committed to following Jesus?
2. Do you want to make a public symbol that identifies you with Jesus, saying "This is who I am and this is the life I lead?"

If you're not ready to be baptized just yet, that's okay. There is nobody forcing you or judging you if you don't. Baptism isn't something that you do to just get it done and over with or just because everyone else at camp, conference, or your church is. Baptism is part of the process of discipleship and each person is at a different spot in that process. All we ask is that you search your heart, ask Jesus to speak to you about it, and then decide. Blessing always follows obedience and with each step of obedience we become more and more of who Jesus is making us to be. Either way, each moment—including baptism and the process of deciding to be baptized or not—is part of the process of becoming more like Jesus.

COMMUNION

"While they were eating, Jesus took a loaf of bread, and after blessing it he broke it, gave it to his disciples, and said, 'Take, eat; this is my body.' Then he took a cup, and after giving thanks he gave it to them, saying, 'Drink from it, all of you; for this is my blood of the covenant, which is poured out for many for the forgiveness of sins." Matthew 26:26-28

Jesus loved food. In fact, one of the complaints and criticisms that Jesus faced from His many critics was that He was a "glutton and a drunk." Of course, Jesus was sinless and perfect which means that He didn't eat or drink too much, but He did have a reputation of enjoying a great meal with other people. Meals were an important part of Jesus' ministry. He ate with his followers, He ate with people that nobody else would, He fed hungry crowds, and there is a sense that Jesus hardly ever preached or spoke unless there was food involved. He called Himself **"the bread of life,"** He often incorporated meals into the stories that He told, and He promised that one day His followers would eat and drink with Him **"at my table in my kingdom."**

Jesus loved food.

It's no wonder than that He chose a meal to be the symbol that tells us who He is and what He is about. Like water baptism, communion reminds us what Jesus has done. He offered bread, which was a symbol of His broken body, and He offered wine, a symbol of His blood. These symbols, however, only make sense if we understand the background behind them. What is it that Jesus is symbolizing in this meal?

REMEMBER WELL

When Jesus gave the command to eat the meal and to share communion, He said to His disciples, **"Do this in remembrance of me."** As Christians we come to communion remembering the life, death, and resurrection of Jesus.

There are a lot of things that we like to remember. We remember our first dog and how much we loved that dog and how sad we were when it was hit by a train. We remember our first date, our first kiss and how great it was, and we remember fun times like road trips, waterskiing, and the good old days. And while these are all good things to remember, this isn't the type of remembering that we do at communion.

Communion is a time where we remember the life and work of Jesus in the past and then choose to see how the life and work of Jesus is shaping and changing us right here, right now. It is the type of remembering that gives us the courage and boldness to press on and follow Jesus into the future.

Communion is important to your discipleship because it helps you to remember where you are going.

COMMUNITY

In communion, we're not simply eating a meal; we are eating a meal together. Human beings are not meant to be alone—we're not meant to live in a cave by ourselves as hermits. Rather, our lives are meant to interact with the people around us and with the God who made us.

Communion is a communal meal that we share in the presence of God and with other Christians. As followers of Jesus, it is absolutely vital to our discipleship process that we work out our faith in a community of other Christians. Communion is important to share in because it physically brings us into a community of other Christians.

Unfortunately there are many gatherings of Christians that look more like a social club and cliques of the popular, powerful, trendy, poor, and needy. Part of the act of communion is to destroy the things that divide us. Where there is difference in race, language, gender, or customs, communion draws Christians together despite all of those differences.

Communion is a meant to be a picture of a world without borders; it is meant to draw you into real relationship with God and with others. Communion is an opportunity to stand for community.

FORGIVEN

Have you ever felt not good enough to take communion? It's Sunday morning, communion is being served, and all you can think about is what you did last night. You feel guilty, dirty, and definitely not worthy to take communion— and so you pass and promise yourself, "I'm going to clean myself up. I'm going to become good again."

Sadly, many Christians take this approach to their faith and they think that if they are somehow good enough God will accept them when they take communion. What happens then is that communion becomes a mark of holiness, a personal badge of goodness, and a reward for somehow being super spiritual. The stark reality, however, is that every Christian comes to the communion table as a sinner in need of mercy, forgiveness, and grace.

That's the beauty of communion. It's for broken, screwed-up, and guilty people.

Being a disciple and follower of Jesus puts you on the path towards restoration, healing, and forgiveness. No matter what you did last night, in communion, Jesus is reminding you that you are forgiven.

This means that when you feel least worthy to take communion, it is the time when you must. Communion becomes a time when we search our hearts and we ask for forgiveness. It is a time where we humble ourselves and repent, we grieve our sin, and we ask for forgiveness while forgiving others. When we as sinners approach communion in this way, communion actually becomes a celebration of forgiveness and moves us closer to becoming more like Jesus.

What about you? Have you ever felt not good enough? This might be the perfect opportunity to ask Jesus for forgiveness and then celebrate with communion!

ANTICIPATION

There is something about anticipation that I think humans love. The best stories are the stories full of suspense and anticipation. Snowboarders understand anticipation when they wake up to blue skies and three feet of fresh snow. High school students with a car and a driver's licence anticipate only one thing: summer vacation and the open road.

Anticipation causes an eagerness in us that makes us hope and dream and doodle things on notebooks. Anticipation makes us look at the future and imagine what could be. It helps build our dreams and guides us into our futures and, without it, what would we do?

This is the most exciting element of communion. Anticipation.

Communion is a meal filled with anticipation! Every time that Christians come together to celebrate communion we're saying that good will come. Every time that Christians come to together to celebrate communion we're saying that pain, brokenness, guilt, frustration, disease, addictions, evil, and death will not have the last word. Communion is a celebration of hope and it looks forward to the day when everything that is broken will be made right.

More than that, when we take communion, we declare our participation in making things right. As followers of Jesus it should be very natural that where we see brokenness we work hard to restore and repair. This is why we fight hard to end human trafficking, why we get passionate about bringing clean water to third world countries, and why we reduce, reuse, and recycle as we care for creation like our Creator asked us to.

Communion is anticipation of the good to come and a declaration that says, "I'll do my part to do good right now. I will **STAND** for freedom. I will **STAND** for the oppressed. I will **STAND** for hope. I will **STAND**."

STAND
JOURNAL PAGES

» "In the morning, Lord, you hear my voice; in the morning I lay my requests before you and wait expectantly." Psalm 5:3

How many times have you caught yourself forgetting something? Whether it's something important or not, how many times do you promise yourself that you will never forget that one thing, and then as the day goes on and as time passes, it escapes you forever. The musician who comes up with a funky jingle but never puts it down on paper. The journalist who doesn't write any information down. The man who goes to the grocery store without a grocery list. We are all bound to forget many things at one point or another. The truth is, we can't remember it all. Imagine the ridiculous amount of information that is going through your head each day, each hour, even each minute!

During the forty years the Israelites were in the wilderness, they constantly forgot all of the miracles that God had done for them, providing them with food, water, and protection. But the Israelites kept forgetting God's past provisions, and kept looking to their current problems as a foundation for their walk with the Lord. **As Deuteronomy 4:9 says, "Be careful, and watch yourselves closely so that you do not forget the things your eyes have seen or let them slip from your heart as long as you live."**

Disciples are documenters. So how do we keep **STANDING**? We must be more intentional about holding on to the truth. Journaling and note taking is a great way to seize what God is speaking to you. Journaling helps you record the rich amount of material you will go through in your lifetime. You will be surprised at how much you find yourself looking back upon past things you have journaled. Journaling also helps keep you focused. Many times I have found myself distracted at church, daydreaming, and the next thing I know, I've missed ten minutes of the sermon. Journaling will keep you focused.

Journaling will also influence those around you. If you were taking notes one Sunday, those around you are going to notice, and start to wonder why they aren't taking it as seriously as you are. You will influence those around you in a good way. Journaling also brings self-discipline. It shows that you are coming into God's presence with an expectant heart. God honours expectant hearts— He loves when people expect big things to happen.

Go to your local mall, Wal-Mart or bookstore. Purchase a journal with blank pages, put your name on it, and make it yours. Use it daily for your Bible reading times. Whenever you have an important thought, or if God speaks something to you, write it down. Make it a habit to bring it along to church and youth meetings. You can also write down dreams, personal goals, poems, prayers, podcast notes. Make it yours, use how you want. Use it regularly and you might be surprised to see all that God is speaking to you about in your life.

STAND
BIBLE READING PLANS

» Need help reading the Bible? Reading plans are great resources that will guide you through select verses and stories on specific topics and time ranges. Here are some reading plans that you might be interested in that will help you in your walk with God. More reading plans can easily be found online.

Who is God? 30 days	
☐ He is the Maker of covenants.	@Genesis 9:8-17
☐ He is the Thwarter of Evil Ambition.	@Genesis 11:1-8
☐ He is a Wrestler.	@Genesis 32:22-32
☐ He is the Bestower of Talents.	@Genesis 41:1-39
☐ He is the Master of the Unexpected.	@Exodus 3:1-17
☐ He is the Protector of the Faithful.	@Exodus 12:1-30
☐ He is the Caterer par Excellence.	@Exodus 16:1-18
☐ He is the Lawgiver.	@Exodus 20:1-21
☐ He is the Punisher of Rebellion.	@Numbers 14:1-45
☐ He is the Opener of Eyes.	@Numbers 22:21-41
☐ He is the Initiator of Vengeance.	@Numbers 31:1-24
☐ He is the One and Only.	@Deuteronomy 4:32-40
☐ He is the Sole Object of Worship.	@Deuteronomy 13:1-18
☐ He is the Offerer of Proof.	@Judges 6:1-40
☐ He is the Protector of Widows.	@Ruth 4:1-12
☐ He is the Hearer of Prayers.	@1 Samuel 1:1-28
☐ He is the Late Night Caller.	@1 Samuel 3:1-21
☐ He is the Rejecter of the Unfaithful.	@1 Samuel 15:1-29
☐ He is the Supporter of the Underdog.	@1 Samuel 17:1-54
☐ He is the Provider of Wisdom.	@1 Kings 3:1-15
☐ He is the Sustainer.	@1 Kings 17:1-24
☐ He is the Undefeated Competitor.	@1 Kings 18:16-40
☐ He is the Gentle Whisperer.	@1 Kings 19:9-18
☐ He is the Orchestrator of Perfect Justice.	@Esther 6:1-7:10

☐	He is the Holder of Satan's Reins.	@Job 1:1-12
☐	He is the Rewarder of Faithfulness.	@Job 42:7-17
☐	He is our Refuge.	@Psalm 18:1-50
☐	He is our Shepherd.	@Psalm 23:1-6
☐	He is the Originator of Prophecy.	@Isaiah 53:1-12
☐	He is the Provider of Salvation.	@John 3

Two Weeks on Becoming a Christian

☐	The first sin creates a need.	@Genesis 3
☐	Salvation prophesied.	@Isaiah 52
☐	The role of the suffering servant.	@Isaiah 53
☐	Three stories about God's love.	@Luke 15
☐	Jesus explains "born again".	@John 3
☐	The good shepherd.	@John 10
☐	Conversions spread outside the Jews.	@Acts 8
☐	Paul testifies of his conversion before a king.	@Acts 26
☐	God's provision for sin.	@Romans 3
☐	Peace with God.	@Romans 5
☐	Salvation unavailable by obeying the law.	@Galatians 3
☐	New life in Christ.	@Ephesians 2
☐	Future rewards of salvation.	@1 Peter 1
☐	Making your salvation pure.	@2 Peter 1

Two Weeks on the Life and Teachings of Jesus

☐	Preparing for Jesus' arrival.	@Luke 1
☐	The story of Jesus' birth.	@Luke 2
☐	The beginning of Jesus' ministry.	@Mark 1
☐	A day in the life of Jesus.	@Mark 9
☐	The Sermon on the Mount.	@Matthew 5

☐	The Sermon on the Mount.	@Matthew 6
☐	Parables of Jesus.	@Luke 15
☐	A conversation with Jesus.	@John 3
☐	Jesus' final instructions.	@John 14
☐	Betrayal and arrest.	@Matthew 26
☐	Jesus' execution on a cross.	@Matthew 27
☐	Resurrection.	@John 20
☐	Jesus' appearance after resurrection.	@Luke 24

The New Testament in 30 Weeks

☐	Week 1	@Matthew 1-9
☐	Week 2	@Matthew 10-19
☐	Week 3	@Matthew 20-28
☐	Week 4	@Mark 1-8
☐	Week 5	@Mark 9-16
☐	Week 6	@Luke 1-8
☐	Week 7	@Luke 9-17
☐	Week 8	@Luke 18-24
☐	Week 9	@John 1-10
☐	Week 10	@John 11-21
☐	Week 11	@Acts 1-10
☐	Week 12	@Acts 11-20
☐	Week 13	@Acts 21-28
☐	Week 14	@Romans 1-8
☐	Week 15	@Romans 9-16
☐	Week 16	@1 Corinthians 1-8
☐	Week 17	@1 Corinthians 9-16
☐	Week 18	@2 Corinthians
☐	Week 19	@Galatians
☐	Week 20	@Ephesians

☐	Week 21	@Philippians & Colossians
☐	Week 22	@1 & 2 Thessalonians
☐	Week 23	@1 & 2 Timothy
☐	Week 24	@Titus & Philemon & Hebrews 1-5
☐	Week 25	@Hebrews 6-13 & James
☐	Week 26	@1 & 2 Peter
☐	Week 27	@1, 2, 3 John & Jude
☐	Week 28	@Revelation 1-6
☐	Week 29	@Revelation 7-14
☐	Week 30	@Revelation 15-22

Major Events in the Bible in 70 Days

☐	Day 1	@Genesis 1
☐	Day 2	@Genesis 2
☐	Day 3	@Genesis 3
☐	Day 4	@Job 38
☐	Day 5	@Romans 1
☐	Day 6	@Genesis 12
☐	Day 7	@Genesis 15
☐	Day 8	@Genesis 21
☐	Day 9	@Genesis 22
☐	Day 10	@Genesis 24
☐	Day 11	@Exodus 1
☐	Day 12	@Exodus 12
☐	Day 13	@Exodus 14
☐	Day 14	@Exodus 16
☐	Day 15	@Exodus 20
☐	Day 16	@Deuteronomy 31

☐	Day 17		@Joshua 1
☐	Day 18		@Joshua 6
☐	Day 19		@Joshua 10
☐	Day 20		@Joshua 24
☐	Day 21		@Judges 2
☐	Day 22		@Judges 4
☐	Day 23		@Judges 16
☐	Day 24		@1 Samuel 3
☐	Day 25		@1 Samuel 8
☐	Day 26		@1 Samuel 13
☐	Day 27		@1 Samuel 17
☐	Day 28		@2 Samuel 5
☐	Day 29		@2 Samuel 7
☐	Day 30		@1 Kings 2
☐	Day 31		@1 Kings 12
☐	Day 32		@1 Kings 16
☐	Day 33		@2 Kings 5
☐	Day 34		@Hosea 11
☐	Day 35		@2 Kings 17
☐	Day 36		@2 Chronicles 13
☐	Day 37		@2 Chronicles 14
☐	Day 38		@2 Chronicles 32
☐	Day 39		@Isaiah 39
☐	Day 40		@2 Kings 24
☐	Day 41		@Jeremiah 25
☐	Day 42		@Jeremiah 29
☐	Day 43		@Daniel 1
☐	Day 44		@Daniel 3
☐	Day 45		@Daniel 6
☐	Day 46		@1 Zechariah 1

☐	Day 47	@Haggai 1
☐	Day 48	@Ezra 1
☐	Day 49	@Ezra 3
☐	Day 50	@Nehemiah 2
☐	Day 51	@Luke 2
☐	Day 52	@Matthew 4
☐	Day 53	@John 4
☐	Day 54	@Matthew 12
☐	Day 55	@Mark 15
☐	Day 56	@Acts 1
☐	Day 57	@Acts 13
☐	Day 58	@Romans 12
☐	Day 59	@2 Timothy 2
☐	Day 60	@1 John 5
☐	Day 61	@Daniel 12
☐	Day 62	@Matthew 24
☐	Day 63	@Revelation 19
☐	Day 64	@Revelation 20
☐	Day 65	@Revelation 21
☐	Day 66	@Psalm 119: 1-32
☐	Day 67	@Psalm 119: 33-64
☐	Day 68	@1 Corinthians 2
☐	Day 69	@2 Timothy 3
☐	Day 70	@2 Peter 1

ABOUT
THE AUTHORS

BEN JOHNSON

Ben Johnson is a passionate leader whose desire is to see God move powerfully in this generation. He serves as NGM (Next Generation Ministries) Director with the Pentecostal Assemblies of Canada, BC and Yukon District. He loves coaching and training leaders, and reaching young people for Christ. Every year, Ben directs several conferences and events, including BC's largest annual youth conference, Historymaker. God has used him to see and set vision, to build young leaders, and to establish pioneering Kingdom initiatives. He and his wife Heather have been married since 1995 and together they live in Langley, BC, with their four children. Find Ben on: Twitter **@benC_johnson**, and check out: **www.nextgenerationministries.ca** and **www.historymaker.ca.**

JEREMY POSTAL

Jeremy Postal serves as a Mission Canada missionary and the director of Whistler School, a bible and discipleship school in beautiful Whistler, BC. He is passionate about building communities of discipleship and mission that are restorative, creative, and focused on the cause and mission of the Gospel. Jeremy also doubles as a freelance writer and blogger who loves to tell stories and walk side-by-side with the people who make them up. He loves deep powder days on the mountain, rock-climbing road trips to the dusty south, morning coffee right into the afternoon, and he's been known to haunt the halls of Twitter. Find Jeremy online at: **www.jeremypostal.com** and on Twitter **@JeremyPostal.** If you're curious about life and mission in Whistler, check out **www.whistlerschool.com.**

STAND CONTRIBUTORS

We are very thankful for the help of a number of dedicated, in-the-trenches youth workers from around British Columbia and Alberta, who generously donated their time and talent by adding valuable portions to this book. Connie Jakab, author of the Culture Rebel blog and book series **(www. culturerebel.com)** contributed three sections: **STAND** as a Woman, **STAND** in Healing, and **STAND** as a Righteous Rebel. Andy Gabruch, veteran youth pastor and leader extraordinaire, contributed the **STAND** in Leadership piece as well as a few of the devotionals. Other devotional contributions came from the likes of Bryce Edelman, Darin Graham, Jabin Postal, Andrew Evans, Nelia Evans, Amy Olsen, Evan Allnut, Adam Browett, Mike Bidell and Jason Ballard. Thank you to Jordan Bateman for the editing help, and to Hannah Jordan for the superb book design. Also a special thanks to Jamie Arseneau for your contributions and helping get this project kick-started. We are so thankful for the many hard-working and dedicated youth workers serving teenagers across BC and the Yukon. We genuinely hope that this will be a great resource for both you and the students you serve.

REFLECTIONS & NOTES

Use these pages to write down your reflections, notes, and prayers.